Longman Structural Readers: Fiction
Stage 4

12

Gold Robbery
and
Mine Mystery

D1808441

Richard Musman

Illustrated by Roger Payne

Longman

Longman Group Limited
London

Associated companies, branches and representatives
throughout the world

© Longman Group Ltd 1972

*First published *1972*
*New impressions *1972; *1973; *1974; *1975*
New impression (with corrections) 1976

ISBN 0 582 53749 5

Acknowledgements

We are grateful to the following for permission to reproduce the photographs:

Barnaby's Picture Library for page 43; Camera Press, London for page 36;
London Express News and Feature Service for page 2; David Mortimer for
page 19.

Map by Brian Lee

Printed in Hong Kong by
Dai Nippon Printing Co., (H.K.) Ltd.

Gold Robbery

Chapter 1

Joe Brook spent the day at the *Daily News* office in front of a telephone. He sat there while the *Daily News* man in New York sent him reports of the gold robbery. That was not the way Joe liked to write stories. He hated to sit at a desk.

As soon as the first news of the robbery reached Fleet Street, he had gone to see his editor, Dick Clegg.

'Send me to New York, Dick,' he said. 'Now!'

But Dick Clegg had refused to send him straight to New York. Joe was angry. Many people bought the *Daily News* just to read Joe's stories. No reporter in England had had so many unusual adventures. Joe had given help to the police of many countries. He had also caused a lot of trouble. Fireman had saved him from the top of a burning New York skyscraper. Indians in Bengal had pulled him from under the feet of a mad elephant. Joe Brook never thought

A London newspaper office.

about danger when there was a good story.

He was still angry when he arrived home in the evening. He looked at the pictures on the walls of his comfortable Kensington flat. There were many photographs of his admirers. There was Danielle Merveille, the famous film star; he had saved her from a snake when it was only six inches from her. There were five small Japanese schoolgirls; he had saved them during an earthquake. There were also pictures of famous criminals; the police had caught them with Joe's help.

He would like to add the gold robbers to these pictures. He looked out of the window. It was wet and cold. The rain was falling heavily. January in England! 'And I could be in the sun in Louisiana!' he thought. He poured out a drink for himself, sat down in a chair and turned on the radio. 'The time is six o'clock,' the familiar voice said. 'Here is the news. The gold robbery——' Joe turned it off angrily. At that moment the telephone rang. He jumped up.

'Bob Slattery speaking,' a voice said quickly. 'I must see you, Joe. I'm at London Airport. I'll be at your flat as soon as I can.'

Bob Slattery was one of Joe's oldest friends. He worked for a bridge-building company and travelled to many parts of the world. Only two weeks before he had sent Joe a card from New Orleans. He had written about the 'good food and kind hearts of the Southerners'. But he had not said that he was in any trouble or danger. Joe could smell a good story. He was excited.

Bob Slattery arrived by taxi half an hour later. Joe could see immediately that something had happened. Bob didn't even say 'hullo'. He put down his suitcase, went straight to the window and pulled back the curtain with great care.

'Look, Joe,' he said, pointing down into the street. 'You see that car—the Jaguar that's parked behind your Aston Martin? Well, it followed my taxi all the way from the airport.'

'Do you know who's driving it?' asked Joe.

'I think so,' Bob said slowly. He took out a cigarette and lit it. Joe noticed that his hand was shaking. 'I think it's one of the gold robbers gang.'

'What!' cried Joe.

'I can't be certain, of course,' Bob continued. 'But I found a strange object in New Orleans two days ago. Since that, *someone* has been following me like a shadow.'

'Two days ago—the day before the gold robbery!' Joe cried. 'Would you recognise him—the man in the Jaguar, I mean?'

'No. I've never seen his face—he's too clever. But I think there are two or three of them, and I'm sure they all have guns. I can tell you, Joe, I'm not often afraid, but I'm afraid now.'

'Have a drink,' said Joe.

Bob poured out a large whisky. He drank half of it immediately. Then he picked up his suitcase, opened it and took out a small metal object. He gave it to Joe.

'That's the thing they want,' he said.

'A model of the Empire State Building!' said Joe, surprised.

'Yes,' Bob said. 'But look at it closely.'

Joe did so. It was quite small, but very heavy. It was covered with nickel. The metal under it was yellow and shone brightly.

'Gold!' Joe cried.

'Yes, gold,' said Bob. 'Our friends in the Jaguar want to get it back. And now you know the reason.'

Joe went to the window and looked between the curtains. The Jaguar had not moved. He could not see the driver. Were the gangsters still in the car or were they hiding in the shadows of the gardens near the road? Joe poured out a drink for himself and sat down beside his friend. The model of the Empire State Building stood on the table in front of them. Joe gave it a long look.

'Where did you find it, Bob?'

'In the French Quarter,' Bob replied. 'I was walking slowly through the narrow old streets. Suddenly I noticed a bright object at the side of the road. I stopped and picked it up. It was the model, of course.'

'And you saw immediately that it was made of gold?'

'Yes. I know a lot about metals. I rubbed some of the nickel off the bottom, and cried out in surprise. A policeman stopped and asked if something was wrong. I showed him the model. "I think it's made of gold," I said. He laughed. "You don't find gold in the streets!" he

Joe gave it a long look.

said. "But if you want to find out, take it to that goldsmith's shop over there!"'

'And the goldsmith said that you were right?' asked Joe.

'No, he didn't!' replied Bob. 'After one quick look at it he said that it was brass covered with nickel. I was surprised, and I looked at his face. It was very white, and he was shaking. "Well, I'll have to take it to a different shop then, won't I?" I said. And I picked up the model. I was just going to leave the shop when he called me back. "I'll give you fifty dollars for it," he said. The policeman had followed me into the shop. "Fifty dollars!" he cried. "That's a lot of money!" "I know a man who collects them," the goldsmith explained quickly.'

'What did he do when you refused his offer?' asked Joe.

'His hand went straight to his pocket. I'm sure he had a gun. But he didn't bring it out because the policeman was there.'

'Would you recognise the man?'

'No. I don't think I would. But I can remember that he spoke like a Frenchman.'

'That's not unusual in New Orleans,' said Joe. 'And the shop? Can you remember that?'

'The shop! Yes, I'd remember the shop. It was very strange. There was no name over the door. It was old and dirty. There was very little for sale. The cases were empty and covered with dust. A smell of machine-oil came from the back rooms. I couldn't see the yard because there was a thick curtain across the side window.'

'Didn't you say anything to the policeman?'

'No. He hadn't noticed anything. When we went out of the shop, he was talking about a baseball game! But I could hear voices in the back of the shop. They were clearly very worried. Then after the policeman had gone, I looked back; I saw a man come out of the door and run down a side street. I'm quite certain that somebody has been following me since that moment.'

'And you said *nothing* to the police?' Joe cried.

'There wasn't time. I jumped into the first taxi, went to my hotel and then to the airport. I wasn't going to stay in New Orleans and allow gangsters to kill me.'

'When did you learn about the gold robbery?'

'This evening when I reached London Airport. I read your report in the *News*.'

'Then why didn't you go immediately to Scotland Yard?'

Bob Slattery finished his glass of whisky and looked Joe straight in the eyes. 'Would *you* have gone to the police, Joe? I'm sure you wouldn't. If I went to Scotland Yard, my "shadow" would know. Then he'd hide, and we'd miss our chance. Now we can catch him *and* the rest of the gang. And we can do it together.'

Joe jumped up. His eyes were shining.

'Where are you going from here, Bob?' he asked.

'To my club in Pall Mall.'

'I'll telephone for a taxi,' said Joe. 'You'd better go to your club and stay there. I'll follow your shadow. If you haven't had a message from me before 9 o'clock tomorrow morning, ring Scotland Yard.'

Chapter 2

The taxi arrived at 7.30, and the driver rang the bell. Joe looked out of the window.

'Wait, Bob,' he said. 'I can see two policemen. Get into the taxi while they are passing the house. Then our friends in the Jaguar won't dare to try anything.'

Two minutes later the policemen passed. Bob jumped quickly into the taxi. Joe heard it drive away. Almost immediately he heard another car. He knew it was the Jaguar. Joe waited for a few seconds. He did not want Bob's 'shadow' to see him. When at last he opened the door, the Jaguar was just disappearing round the corner at the end of the road.

He looked across the street at the dark gardens. He could not see anything among the trees, and he could hear nothing except the sound of the rain. He jumped into his Aston Martin and drove off towards the West End. He looked behind him. No one was following him. He parked his car in a side street near Piccadilly and walked down to Pall Mall. To his surprise, the Jaguar was parked only twenty yards from the front door of the club. He could see three men inside the car.

Joe hid in the dark shadows a few yards from the door of the club. It was still raining. He took out his favourite pipe and filled it with strong, black tobacco. He was wearing his thick leather coat, and he did not notice the cold or the rain.

He smoked three pipes. Well-dressed men went in and out of the club. Cars, taxis and the big red London buses passed one after another. Groups of people walked quickly along the pavement under their umbrellas. But the doors of the Jaguar did not open.

It was 10.30. Joe had just filled his fourth pipe when a taxi stopped right in front of him. A girl in a short skirt got out. She was very beautiful—about 25, perhaps. Her face was dark, but she had long fair hair. She took one step on the wet pavement, slipped and fell. Joe completely forgot the Jaguar. He ran forward. But a man in a fur coat got there first. Joe stopped. The man—Joe could only see his back—offered the girl his hand. She got up slowly. There was a cut below her left ear, but she did not seem to be badly hurt. She took a handkerchief out of her bag and put it to the cut. Then she said something to the man and walked quickly away towards Trafalgar Square. The man seemed surprised—almost angry. 'Women!' he said. Then suddenly he turned and went straight up to the Jaguar. A head appeared at the car window. The man in the fur coat said something, and a violent quarrel started. At last the car door opened, and a little man in a black coat got out.

'I can't do it, Carlo!' cried the little man. 'She——'

'Be quiet!' said the man in the fur coat. 'I know better than a woman!'

They continued to talk angrily in low voices. Then the little man walked quickly up to the doorman of the club. He was carrying a case. It was the kind of case that business men use for their papers. But its shape showed that there was a large heavy object inside it. Joe was suddenly worried. 'Will the doorman remember Bob's orders?' he wondered. 'Will he keep the little man out?' Joe waited. He heard the little man say in a loud voice:

'I'm a friend of Mr Slattery.'

'I'm sorry, sir,' replied the doorman. 'Mr Slattery can see no one tonight.'

'But he's waiting for me,' said the little man. 'I must see him.'

'I'm sorry, sir,' the doorman repeated. 'He's busy.'

The little man went back to the Jaguar and started to quarrel again with Carlo. For a moment, Joe thought that the two men were going to fight. Carlo kicked the little man hard, so that he cried out with pain. But they did not shout, and Joe could not hear a word. At last the little man got back into the Jaguar and shut the door violently. Carlo lit a cigar, took one last look at the club door and walked away towards Piccadilly.

Joe decided quickly. He went after Carlo.

Carlo walked fast up the Haymarket towards Piccadilly Circus. Joe stayed ten yards or more behind him. Carlo did not look round, but after a few minutes he threw his cigar into the road and put both his hands into his pockets. 'Has he got *two* guns?' Joe wondered.

At the steps which go down to the Underground, Carlo stopped.

7

Joe hoped that he would look round. He wanted to see his face. But the man suddenly ran down the steps and disappeared. Joe ran after him. The big round hall under Piccadilly Circus was full of people. Joe searched among the crowd. 'I've lost him,' he said to himself angrily. At that moment he suddenly saw him again. Carlo was leaving by one of the passages on the other side of the hall. Did he know that somebody was following him?

Joe went after him. Piccadilly Circus was full of Scotsmen who had travelled to London for the big football game against England at Wembley the next day. They were laughing and singing. The police were asking them to move, but they took no notice.

Carlo pushed through the crowd and into the dark streets of Soho. Soho lies to the north of Piccadilly Circus. It is a strange—and sometimes dangerous—part of London. It is famous for its foreign restaurants and also for its night-clubs.

Carlo was walking quickly again. Both his hands were deep in his pockets. There were fewer people in the streets here. The night-clubs were open, but most of the restaurants were shut and had turned off

The passage was very narrow and quite empty.

their lights. Men stood in the shadows of the narrow streets and moved away when policemen appeared.

Suddenly Carlo turned into a dark passage. The passage was very narrow and quite empty. The few doors were shut, and there were no lights in the windows. Joe was angry with himself. He had left his stick at home. Joe's heavy stick had saved his life more than once. He usually took it with him at times like this.

Joe looked down at his hands. They were big and strong—and hard. 'If I can get near enough——' he said to himself. Then he went into the passage. Clearly Carlo had heard him coming. He began to run. Joe began to run too. Suddenly Carlo came to a corner. He stopped and turned round. At the same time, a light went on in a room on the ground floor, and for the first time Joe saw Carlo's face. He had never seen an uglier face in all his life. The man had no hair, and a scar ran right across his face.

A knife flew through the air.

Joe just had time to jump to one side. He felt a sudden pain in his right arm. He fell back, and heard the knife land in the wood of a

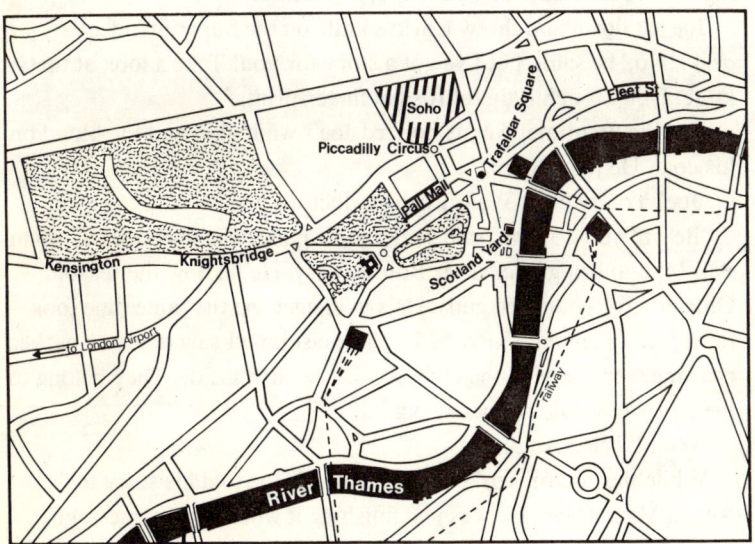

Central London.

door behind him. He found that he could not move his arm. The knife had gone through the thick leather of his coat and held him there.

He took out his handkerchief and put it round the knife. He did not want to destroy any finger-prints. Then he pulled himself free and ran on down the passage. Carlo had disappeared.

Joe did not stop to look at his wound. He was sure that it was not bad. As soon as he reached the street, he stopped a taxi.

'Scotland Yard,' he told the driver. 'And hurry!'

Chapter 3

As soon as Joe reached Scotland Yard, he asked to see Chief Superintendent Macfarlane. Angus Macfarlane was one of England's most famous detectives. Joe had often been able to help him, and each of the two men liked and respected the other.

'Well, Joe,' said Angus, 'what brings you here at this time of the night? I've no story for you today, I'm afraid.'

Joe sat down and threw Carlo's knife on the Superintendent's desk. 'No,' he said, 'but I've got a story for you! Take a look at that knife. Don't touch it there! It's got finger-prints.'

For the first time, Angus noticed Joe's white face and the blood on his coat. He jumped up.

'Joe! You're hurt. Wait. I'll get a doctor.'

'Before you do that,' said Joe, 'send a police car to Block's Club in Pall Mall to bring back a Mr Bob Slattery. He'll know the reason. Oh, and give your men guns. He's in danger. At the same time look for a green Jaguar—XBZ 527 E. The last time I saw it, it was parked near the front door of the club. Arrest the men inside. They belong to the American gold robbers gang.'

'What!' cried Angus.

While the doctor worked on his wound, Joe told his story to Angus Macfarlane. He was just finishing it when a radio message arrived from the police officer in Pall Mall. The Jaguar, of course, had disappeared. Angus immediately sent out a description of the

Jaguar, and of Carlo, to every police car and every police officer in the country.

'We'll search Soho,' he said. 'But we'll find nothing. These men are too clever. They'll soon be on their way back to New Orleans in their own plane!'

Ten minutes later, Bob Slattery walked into the Superintendent's office. Angus Macfarlane took one look at the gold model and sent it to the laboratory. The laboratory report came back immediately. The model had indeed been made from part of a Mexican gold bar.

Angus picked up the telephone. 'Get me the FBI, Washington,' he said.

Angus Macfarlane's telephone conversation with Washington explained a lot. 'Carlo', they learnt, was quite clearly Carlo Menodotti, a well-known gangster.

'The FBI want Menodotti,' Angus explained. 'They want him for robbery—*and* worse crimes. They are sure that Menodotti is a killer. Three hours before you left New Orleans, the FBI men found him in a small restaurant in the poor part of the city. He was sitting alone at

The F.B.I. agents burst in to the restaurant.

a table, but he wasn't eating. It was clear that he was waiting for somebody. He hadn't noticed the FBI agents, so they hid behind a door and watched. A few moments later, a well-dressed man came into the restaurant and sat down at Carlo's table. Carlo asked immediately, "Is Rosa Santos coming?" The man replied, "Yes, in a minute." Then suddenly a waiter ran in and said something in Carlo Menodotti's ear. Carlo and his friend jumped up and ran into the back of the restaurant. The FBI men pulled out their guns and ran after them. They searched the house. They found nothing. The man who owned the restaurant, the waiters—everybody had disappeared.'

'Do the FBI know the name of Carlo's friend?' asked Joe.

'Yes,' said Angus. 'His name is Hyman Dixon. He owns ships and is a very rich man. The police went immediately to Dixon's house, but it was too late. There was nobody there. They found nothing.'

'And Rosa Santos?' asked Joe.

'That's strange,' Angus said. 'Hyman has no wife and no sisters. His friends say that he hates women.' Angus looked at his notes. 'But the FBI have discovered one important fact. Hyman Dixon often used to go to Mexico City. He always stayed at the same hotel. A waiter in the hotel once saw Dixon and a dark-haired woman together in a quiet part of the garden. He says that the woman was beautiful, but he can't give a full description of her.'

'The mystery of the dark-haired lady!' said Joe.

'Yes. The FBI and the Mexican Police have had a very important conversation about this "mystery lady". The Mexican Police think she's head of a big gang in Mexico City. The FBI now think——'

'—that she and Hyman Dixon are the heads of the gold robbers gang!' cried Joe.

'Yes,' said Angus, 'and they also think that Dixon and Santos sent Menodotti to deal with Mr Slattery.'

Joe jumped up.

'Well,' he cried. 'I'm going to telephone Dick Clegg! He can't refuse to send me to New Orleans *now*.'

Angus put out his hand and stopped Joe. 'Your arm, Joe. It's not hurting you too much?'

Joe's wound *was* hurting him, but he laughed. 'It's nothing!' he said. 'You know *me*, Angus!'

Angus smiled. 'I know you very well,' he said. Then he turned to Bob Slattery. 'And you, sir—would you agree to go back to New Orleans if necessary?'

'Me!' said Bob. 'Why do they want me?'

'They need you because you saw the goldsmith.'

'Good!' cried Joe. 'Then we can travel together.'

'Wait, Joe,' said Angus Macfarlane. 'I've told you that Menodotti is a killer. But there's another thing that I haven't told you. Menodotti hates to fail. Well, he failed in Soho. He didn't kill you!'

'Ah!' said Joe. 'So, if Carlo sees me walking through the streets of New Orleans——'

'That's right,' said Angus. 'The FBI think he'll try again.'

'Telephone London Airport immediately!' said Joe.

Two days later, when Joe was quite well again, he and Bob were on the first plane to New York. From there they flew straight to New Orleans. A special agent of the FBI met them at the airport.

'Max Pressburger,' the FBI agent said. 'Glad to know you, gentlemen.'

Max Pressburger was a large man with a square face. His fair hair was very short, and his white shirt was open at the neck.

'Better weather than in London, I'm sure,' he said.

The two Englishmen agreed. The sun shone from a clear blue sky, but it was not too hot. The plane had come to a stop almost half a mile from the airport buildings. A car with thick glass windows was waiting.

'We must take great care,' Max Pressburger explained. 'I've brought bullet-proof vests for you too. When Menodotti shoots, he doesn't often miss. And he always aims at the heart.'

They drove down long roads in the shade of tall trees. Even in January, the gardens of the large, brightly painted houses were full of flowering bushes and trees. There were no fences between the houses and no front gates. 'It's more friendly than in England,' Joe thought. At one of the biggest houses they saw policemen on the grass and on the sidewalk.

'That's Hyman Dixon's place,' said Max.

13

They turned into Canal Street, the busy heart of New Orleans. After a few blocks, they turned again and drove to the City Police building in the French Quarter. 'We won't get a very warm welcome,' Max told them. 'The City Police don't like the FBI. They think we want to destroy their independence.'

This time Max was wrong. The Police Chief was glad to see the FBI agent. One of his policemen had just disappeared.

'He was walking down the street just two blocks away,' the Police Chief said. 'Suddenly a car stopped beside him. A door opened, and he was pulled inside. Then the car drove away very fast.'

'That's Menodotti's work,' Max said.

Joe looked at Bob quickly.

'It could be the policeman who took me to the goldsmith's shop,' said Bob.

'Have you got a picture of him?' Max asked the Police Chief.

'Sure! He's a nice guy. Has a wife and two kids.'

The Police Chief threw a photograph on his desk. It was a few years old. The policeman was standing in the middle of his family. He was not wearing his uniform, but Bob recognised him immediately.

'That's him,' he said.

The Police Chief and Max could not hide their surprise.

'Well!' cried the Police Chief.

'Do you think you could find the goldsmith's shop again, Mr Slattery?' asked Max.

'Yes, I think so,' replied Bob. 'It was near Antoine's—not more than five minutes' walk from the restaurant.'

'Let's go!' said Max.

Joe, Bob and Max got back into the bullet-proof car of the FBI. The Police Chief, with two other cars and six policemen, went too. The policemen all had guns. They drove straight to Antoine's, and from there Bob found the goldsmith's shop without difficulty. It was shut. There were boards across the windows and the door. The tall gates of the yard were locked.

Max spoke over the radio to the Police Chief in the car behind. 'Don't move yet. Carlo may be inside.'

At that moment Joe noticed something on the flat roof of a building across the road—something which shone in the sunlight. He turned to Max.

'I think Carlo is up there,' he said. 'I can see a gun.'

Max looked at the roof through his field-glasses.

'No,' he said. 'It's not a gun. It's a piece of metal. But I'll search the building.'

The building was empty. Three policemen searched it from top to bottom. A policeman also climbed on to the roof. They found nothing.

'Good!' said Max. 'Now we'll go into the goldsmith's shop. But you, Mr Brook, will you please walk behind us. It's my duty to look after you. If Carlo *is* inside, he'll aim at *you*.'

They all got out of the cars and moved slowly towards the shop. Suddenly Joe stopped, turned round and looked up at the roof again. Immediately a gun fired. He did not have time to move. The bullet hit the bullet-proof vest above his heart. The force of the bullet knocked him backwards. At the same time the police opened fire and rushed into the building. But it was too late. Carlo Menodotti had disappeared across the roof-tops.

'So you were right!' said Max. 'Menodotti was hiding there all the time.'

Chapter 4

There was a heavy lock on the door of the goldsmith's shop. The Police Chief fired his gun into the lock, and opened the door. The policemen went in. Two other policemen broke down the gates of the yard. There was no one inside the shop, and the yard was empty.

Clearly the gang had left in a great hurry. Bob Slattery looked around him with surprise.

'They haven't even emptied the glass cases,' he cried. 'But the smell of machine-oil is even stronger today. Look! That door over there! It's open.'

He ran towards it.

'Stop!' ordered Max. 'Somebody may be in there with a gun.'

Then he turned to the waiting policemen. 'Follow me,' he said.

A dark passage led to some steps. At the bottom of the steps there was an open door. When Max reached the top of the steps, he stopped and called to a policeman behind him. The policeman was carrying a special gun. Max ordered him to point the gun down the steps. Then he shouted, 'Come out, or we'll use gas! I'll count to ten.'

Max counted to ten. There was no answer from below, no sound at all.

'We'll go in,' said Max after a few seconds. 'I don't think there's anyone there.'

Max and the Police Chief went in first. The policemen followed and, last of all, Joe and Bob. Suddenly they all stopped, and even Max cried out in surprise. They were in the gold robbers' workshop. There were large piles of nickel. There was gold dust over everything. And there were dozens of moulds of the Empire State Building.

It was Joe who discovered the first gold bar. He found it in a dark corner of the passage which led to the yard. The policemen who were searching the yard found two more bars.

'The question is,' said the Police Chief, 'where are the rest of the bars?'

'On a boat!' said Max. 'I'm sure of it.'

'Well then,' said the Police Chief unhappily, 'it will be very hard to find them. There's water all round this city—the Mississippi, the lakes, all the small rivers— Where do we start?'

'The docks,' replied Max. 'Our reports show that thousands of models of the Empire State Building have left New Orleans by sea during the last two years. The gang have been able to send their treasure out of America quite openly. Now they'll have to hide it.'

'We'll have to search every ship in the docks,' cried the Police Chief. 'And not only the ships which are going down the Mississippi to the sea. We'll have to search every ship which is sailing up the Mississippi too.'

'You're right,' said Max. 'Dixon's clever. He could take the gold to Chicago and the Great Lakes and on to Canada. We must hurry.'

A large crowd was waiting outside the goldsmith's shop. Joe looked at the people with interest. Tourists were busy with their cameras. Groups of Negroes stood apart and talked excitedly. There were men with fair hair. There were people with black hair who spoke Spanish. Many of the girls were beautiful. He noticed one especially. She had short black hair. Her dark face was very beautiful, but very hard, Joe thought. She was wearing a blue cotton dress. Suddenly Joe noticed that she had a piece of sticking-plaster below her left ear. He looked at the girl's face again—with great care. Then he turned to Max.

'That girl over there,' he said. 'Do you know her?'

Max looked. 'No, I'm afraid not,' he said. 'Why?'

Joe was excited. 'I saw her three days ago in London,' he began. 'She had long fair hair then. But I'm sure it's the same girl. The shape of her face, the sticking-plaster——'

Suddenly a gun was fired, and a policeman shouted, 'There's Menodotti!'

Max left Joe immediately and ran towards the policeman. It was

. . . she had a piece of sticking-plaster below her left ear.

not Menodotti. But before Max returned, the girl had disappeared among the crowd. Joe did not wait. He ran after the girl. At first he thought that he had lost her, but he soon saw the blue dress again. Rosa—he was sure it was Rosa—was walking quickly in the shade of the old houses. Joe wondered if Hyman Dixon was waiting in one of them. But Rosa did not stop. She passed old Spanish archways. Through them Joe could see gardens full of flowers and tall trees. Perhaps Hyman was waiting in one of these cool gardens.

Rosa walked straight on. She reached the French Market. People were drinking coffee there outside the cafés. Artists were sitting and standing on the sidewalk. Rosa knocked one artist's picture as she passed. The man shouted something at her, but she took no notice.

At last she turned towards the river. Joe could already smell the river, and soon he had his first view of it—the great wide brown Mississippi, the longest river in the world. In the distance he could see the great new motor bridge. The ships which passed under it seemed like toys.

Rosa stopped when she reached the river. She seemed worried.

A street in the French Quarter.

She looked around her, and Joe quickly hid behind a car. A taxi passed, and almost stopped when the driver saw her. But Rosa shook her head. When the road was quite clear, she ran to a small motor-boat. She looked down into the boat, called a name and then jumped on board.

'What do I do now?' Joe said to himself. But he did not have to worry. Rosa appeared again immediately. She was looking at her watch, and she seemed very angry. She looked up and down the quay. 'She wants to call somebody, but she's afraid,' Joe thought. Then suddenly she noticed a bar at a street corner a few blocks away. She said something. Then she ran like the wind towards the bar.

Joe acted immediately. He started to run too. Two lines of cars were parked along the quay near the boat. He knew that no one could see him from the bar. He jumped on board and went down into the little cabin. He could not hide in the cabin, but at the end of it there was a door. Joe opened it. It was a large cupboard for tools and ropes. Joe climbed into it. There was not much room, but he shut the door behind him and hid himself under a pile of ropes. A few moments later, he heard footsteps, and a man's voice said,

'I hit him this time—right over the heart. He didn't even fall. He isn't a man at all!'

Clearly Carlo was already a little drunk, and Rosa was very angry now. 'Be quiet, you drunken animal!' she said. 'We said "No killing", and twice you've tried to kill Brook—once in London, now here. Mr Dixon will be very angry with you, I promise you. Now move!'

'You're only a woman,' said Carlo. 'I don't listen to women! I'll kill that Englishman, even if——'

'No, you won't,' said Rosa. Her voice was cold, hard and cruel.

'No! Don't shoot!' cried Carlo.

So Rosa had a gun too!—A rope fell into the Mississippi. The engine started. There was a sound of rushing water as the boat left the quay. It was completely dark inside the cupboard, and terribly hot. Joe could breathe only with great difficulty. He had a pain in his right leg, and the heavy ropes hurt his back. The noise of the engine was terrible. 'Am I going to faint?' he wondered. But just then the engine stopped. Someone shouted,

'Here! Catch this rope.'

'Go on! Catch it!' Rosa ordered Carlo. Then Joe heard her say in a low voice, 'They've found the shop, Dixon.'

A voice—clearly a Southerner's—replied, 'Don't worry. They'll find nothing, even if they search us. We're ready to leave. Come on board, both of you.'

Joe waited for a few seconds. Then, with an effort, he got out of the cupboard. From the cabin, he could see that the motor-boat was close to the side of a large ship. The ship was at a quay in the heart of the New Orleans docks.

Joe could reach dry land only by water. He had to swim. He looked up the tall side of the ship. He could see nobody. He took off his bullet-proof vest and dropped it quietly into the Mississippi. Then he climbed over the side of the motor-boat and began to swim under water. He came up three times for air. 'Is somebody going to shoot?' he wondered each time. But nothing happened. Ahead of him he could see a British ship which was loading cotton. A sailor saw him and put a rope over the side. Joe climbed on board.

'Get the police! Be as quick as you can!' he told the sailor.

Ten minutes later, Joe was describing his adventure to Max and the Police Chief. They were searching a ship nearly half a mile away.

'Boy, oh boy!' the Police Chief cried. 'Am I glad to see you, Mr Brook!'

Then he gave orders to his men.

'Dock 47. SS *Freedom*. But take care, boys. They have certainly got guns.'

GOLD ROBBERY - Ships searched
in docks   No sign of gang

The police have now searched the *Freedom* from end to end. They have questioned the captain and all his officers and seamen. The captain is a well known and respected New Orleans man. He carries cotton from New Orleans to Liverpool. The police found no gold and none of the Dixon gang on board.

'Mr Brook has made a mistake,' the captain said. 'Mr Dixon has never visited my ship. I have never even met him.'

But Mr Brook is quite certain that he made no mistake. He described the motor-boat which took him to the docks. This motor-boat has not yet been found.

LATE NEWS

Police have arrested Hyman Dixon, Rosa Santos and all their gang. Gold bars worth one million dollars have been found on the *Freedom*. Joe Brook, the English newspaperman, and two policemen are in hospital. They were wounded in a gunfight on board the ship.

Our reporter talked to the City Police Chief.

'Mr Pressburger and I were sure that Joe Brook's story was true,' the Police Chief said. 'So we hid twenty policemen in the buildings near the *Freedom*. We watched the ship through field-glasses. But we noticed nothing unusual. Joe Brook was with us.

'At 10.55 Joe disappeared. Two minutes later, we saw him running towards the *Freedom*. The ship was just going to sail. Only one rope still held her. We saw Joe climb this rope and jump on board. The captain and some of the men saw him too. Two men seized him.

'Suddenly a gun was fired. Mr Brook fell. At the same time, a hidden door in the funnel opened, and Menodotti rushed out. He was shouting wildly: "I've killed him?"

'My men did not wait for orders. They attacked the *Freedom* immediately. Menodotti opened fire again and hit two of them. My men fired back. Menodotti was hit in the arm and dropped his gun. That was the end of the gunfight because, at that moment, Hyman Dixon walked out of the funnel. He was carrying a white flag.'

The secret room in the funnel was the hiding-place for all the Dixon gang. All the gold was there. And the missing City policeman was a prisoner inside the funnel. The captain and some of the seamen knew the secret. Dixon had paid them well.

Everybody in New Orleans is now wondering: did Joe Brook know that Carlo Menodotti would shoot? Did he go on board the *Freedom* in order to tempt him?

Mr Brook is not badly hurt. But when our reporter questioned him in hospital, he only smiled.

'I'm writing my own story,' he said.

S?

er congressional
year, Mr Green-
would have lost
votes from those
ployed " (a total
illion people in
t seasonal adjust-
2.5 million two

this, Mr Green-
hat fewer than
of October's un-
of voting age
about half of
ligible citizens
n a presidential

n's thesis is that
ritching would
ear of becoming
ich is caused by
rate.

in GNP in 1970
officials in other
inflation now
men scaling the
perhaps 6 per
out double the
nmonly predicted
onomists.

officials estimate
more modest re-
e enough to have
rate down to
cent and 4.5 per
summer of 1972.

s increasing talk
nistration men
d accept a rate
ove 5 per cent
dverse political
as long as it is
a demonstrably
ction.

upport for this
n rather cynical
an Greenspan, a
York economist
s to the admini-
President Nixon
ng for re-election

ase in

Ja
lin

in

Japan
three m
companie
tures wi
textiles i

The p
ment of
Mitsubis
Industrie
ning an
Asahi C
Clarke S

The C
ently ma
medium
textile f
competit
One infl
" Nihon
the Gove
in an att
locked t
tween th

The M
Trade a
that Ja
will me
America
ducts ar
with US

The
the Min
three J
willingne
ventures
expected
applicati

US

The
the Unit
be muc

21

Mine Mystery

Chapter 1

Joe Brook had been in Africa. He had returned only that afternoon. But his editor, Dick Clegg, had hired a special plane for him, and he had flown straight to Cardiff. A car was waiting for him there.

The evening was cold and clear. The city streets were full of people who were returning home. Joe noticed the posters of the evening newspaper—'Pit explosion. Latest news'. People stopped and read the front page.

It was 7 o'clock when he reached Ryddach. It was almost dark, but there were still hundreds of people near the pit gates. They stood quite quietly by the low wall round the mine buildings and watched the rescue teams come out into the fresh air. Others were waiting in anxious, silent groups at the main gate.

The mine lay at the bottom of a deep valley, and on both sides of it the houses of Ryddach stood in rows on the hillsides. Ryddach was

A mining village in South Wales.

the last town in the valley. The wild hills of South Wales lay just beyond it. Joe could see trees on the skyline. The dark coal tip rose like a mountain from the floor of the valley. The tip was so high and so black that Joe did not immediately see the two great winding-towers. The wheel of one of them was turning, bringing up the cage. Who was in the cage? A rescue team? Or some of the trapped miners?

The women in the road began to talk as the men stepped out of the cage. The men's faces were black with coal dust. Some of them could walk only with difficulty. One man was on a stretcher. His mates looked at the women and shook their heads. The women were silent again.

Joe went up to a young woman who was standing alone. He was just going to speak to her, but she spoke first.

'You're not from here, are you?' she said. 'Then you won't understand. All those trapped men live in this town. Ten of them live in one small street.'

'And your husband——?' Joe began.

'Oh, he's all right!'

She spoke so bitterly that Joe looked at her with surprise.

'He escaped,' she said quickly. 'But my brother Dai is still down there. And that girl who is standing near the wall—her husband is Dai's team captain. They live in our street. She had a baby a month ago. You see that old man beside her? He lives on the other side of us. His son was killed during the war. Now his grandson is dead. His body was brought out this morning. If the rescue teams cannot save the trapped men, there will be a hundred children in this town without fathers.'

Joe walked to the main gate, and a policeman allowed him to go in. A group of men were resting near a railway truck. They were still wearing their helmets. One of them had forgotten to turn off his lamp. Rivers of sweat ran down their black faces. Joe stopped and offered them cigarettes.

'You've just come up, haven't you?' he asked.

'Yes,' said one of them. His face was covered with coal dust.

'That's Cliff Williams,' said another man. 'He was down there when it happened, and he was hurt.'

A group of men were resting.

'Only a small cut on my leg,' Cliff Williams said.

'Why did you go down again?' Joe asked.

'Because my mates are still down there!' There was an angry note in Cliff's voice. 'That's why!'

'Can you tell me about it?' Joe asked.

Cliff gave him an unfriendly look. 'You're a newspaperman, aren't you?' he said.

'Yes,' Joe replied. 'I'm Joe Brook.'

'Joe Brook of the *Daily News*?' Cliff said. 'That's different. I'll tell *you*. This morning my mate and I were repairing a machine in the U5 District. At 10.15 we stopped and had something to eat. Suddenly we heard a noise. It was rather like an explosion, but in the distance. We weren't worried. We thought it was at the coal face. You know that explosives are used to break open the coal seams. But a few moments later we felt a rush of air and there was a thick cloud of dust. Then a boy arrived. He told us that there had been an accident in the main roadway of the U4 District. "Come and help. Bring a stretcher," he said.'

Cliff stopped and lit another cigarette. Then he continued.

'We picked up the stretcher and went straight to the roadway. The roof had fallen in. We found a boy dead. He was lying between the tram lines a few feet from the rock fall. A piece of rock had hit him on the back of the head. We put him on the stretcher. We had walked about twenty yards when my mate said, "The roof is moving!" I looked back. I could see the steel arches beginning to bend. We dropped the stretcher and ran for our lives. We were lucky. We were near one of the side roadways when the roof fell. We ran in and threw ourselves flat on our faces. The falling rock and earth just missed our feet. For five minutes the dust was so thick that we couldn't see anything at all. We thought that the side roadway was completely blocked. We thought that we were trapped. But we were just able to climb out. My lamp had broken when I fell. Then a falling stone broke my mate's lamp. It was completely dark then. We climbed down the rock fall until we reached the tram lines. There was so much dust that we had difficulty in breathing. We moved inch by inch along the tram lines until the rescue team found us.'

At that moment a doctor called from a building with a red cross sign on its door: 'Come here, Cliff. I want to look at that leg.'

'It's quite all right, Doc,' Cliff cried.

But he went over to the Red Cross building. Joe went to the pit head. Ambulances, rescue team lorries, doctors' and National Coal Board cars stood in rows near the winding-towers. There was a rush of escaping air as the cage took another rescue team into the mine.

Through the noise Joe heard a voice: 'You're Joe Brook, aren't you? I've often seen your photograph in the *News*.'

Joe turned and saw a small man with a thin, intelligent face.

'I'm Gwyn Davies,' the man said. 'I'm the mine secretary. I would be very glad if I could talk to you—alone.'

'Certainly,' Joe said, with surprise.

He followed Gwyn Davies up some steps into the manager's office. A long table filled the centre of the room. The table was covered with papers. It was very hot. A door led into the shower room, and Joe could hear the sound of running water. Gwyn Davies led Joe into a small room and closed the door.

'You know, Mr Brook,' he began, 'that we are having trouble with reporters.'

'I can promise you, Mr Davies———' Joe began.

Gwyn Davies held up his hand. 'I know that you're different, Mr Brook,' he said. 'I haven't brought you here in order to complain. I want to ask for your help.'

They both sat down. As Joe filled his pipe, he noticed a look of deep anxiety on Gwyn Davies's face.

'I started in the pits myself—at the age of fourteen,' Gwyn Davies began. 'That was in the thirties. It was a hard life in those days. There were no cutting machines. I worked with a pick. I could only move forwards on my hands and knees because the roof of the passages was so low. My father was in the mines too. His pay was so small that his family often had nothing to eat. He was still a young man when he died———'

'Why are you telling me all this?' Joe said.

'Because most people have no idea of the life of a miner,' Gwyn replied. 'It is true that the bad days are over. Pay is good today. Miners don't use picks any more. They don't go home black and have a bath in a small tub in the living-room. They walk into the streets from the pit-head baths as clean as you are now. But their lives are still hard and dangerous, Mr Brook———'

Gwyn Davies suddenly stopped and looked Joe straight in the eyes.

'Would it surprise you, Mr Brook, if a miner put his mates in danger by an act of sabotage?'

'Of course!' Joe replied. 'Do you think the newspapers were right, then? Do you think it *was* sabotage?'

'I would like to say no,' Gwyn Davies said. 'Miners are like brothers when they are underground. They very often risk their lives to save their mates. Men who will never talk above ground are friends at the coal face. But not in this pit! Not now!'

'Do you know the reason?'

'The National Coal Board is going to close the pit. The men are worried. Miners love their homes, Mr Brook. They are afraid that they will have to leave the valley. But at Ryddach there is another more worrying reason. There is a trouble-maker in the pit.'

'And you think that this man caused the explosion?'

'I don't know. But he was the nearest man to the explosion, and he escaped. If we can rescue any of the trapped men, perhaps we shall learn the real facts. One thing is certain—the police will ask questions.'

'How can I help you?' Joe asked.

'Visit the man. Talk to him. Try to find out the facts. You'll get more from him than the police will. He'd like to talk to the great Joe Brook—he's that kind of man. He'll tell you a lot of lies, especially about Ivor Evans, the manager. The man doesn't come from a mining family. His father had a shop in Cardiff, but he's married to a miner's daughter. They have an adopted child, a little Polish boy of twelve.'

Gwyn Davies wrote down a name and address on a piece of paper—'Gareth Morgan, 4 Cefn Coed Road'.

'I'm sure you won't say a word of this to anybody,' Gwyn said. 'I'll tell you everything I know about Morgan. I know quite a lot.

'*Do you think it* was *sabotage?*'

You see, I'm secretary to Ivor Evans, and nobody understands
Gareth Morgan better than Ivor Evans!'

Chapter 2

Joe smoked his pipe while Gwyn told him the story of Gareth
Morgan. Gareth had been a trouble-maker at school. He was clever.
He had won a place at a grammar school, and he had usually been
top of his class there. But the teachers did not like him, because
Gareth hated rules. He did not think that it was right to have rules.
He enjoyed power, and he was a bully. The smaller boys feared him.
Most of the older pupils hated him. Only a small group of boys
accepted him as their leader.

Gareth and this gang caused trouble in the school and in the city.
They broke windows, took bicycles, even cars. The police caught
some of the boys, but they never caught Gareth. He was too clever.
When he left school, Gareth surprised everybody. People thought he
would get work in the city. They thought he wanted money. But he
went into the mines.

The miners, young and old, did not like him at all. They were very
angry indeed when he married Lynn, the daughter of Tom Jones.
Everybody in the Ryddach pit loved Tom Jones. But Gareth soon
quarrelled with Tom.

After a few weeks, he formed a gang. He found one or two miners
who hated their work. The gang very soon began to cause trouble in
the pit. There were fights underground, even at the coal face. They
broke trams and conveyor belts—and blamed other miners. Team
captains found it more and more difficult to stop the quarrels.

Nobody could prove that Gareth was the cause of the trouble, not
even Ivor Evans. Gareth hated Ivor Evans. He hated him because he
was quiet and never shouted. Ivor was the only man in the pit who
was not afraid of Gareth. Gareth certainly hated him for that. 'Some
people think he's a little mad,' Gwyn said.

'Did Morgan have other reasons to hate Ivor Evans?' Joe asked.

'Yes,' Gwyn replied. 'Ivor was going to sack him. Now I'll show you the way to Gareth Morgan's house.'

It was quite dark when Joe left the pit. Gwyn Davies said good-bye to him at the gate.

'You can stay the night at my house, if you like,' Gwyn said. He gave Joe his address and went back to the pit head.

Joe walked up the hill to Cefn Coed Road. The women had gone home. The curtains were drawn across the front-room windows. There was a strange silence.

Cefn Coed Road was short. It ended at the bottom of the coal tip. In the weak light of the street lamp, Joe noticed that the bricks of the little houses were black with coal dust, but the doors and windows were brightly painted. He rang the bell of No. 4.

The door was opened by a young woman. Joe recognised her immediately. It was the woman who had spoken to him earlier in the evening. Mrs Morgan was perhaps thirty. She was still pretty, but her face was tired, and her grey eyes were sad.

'Hullo,' Joe said. 'You're Mrs Morgan, aren't you? Is your husband in?'

A mining village street.

29

Before she could answer, an angry voice shouted, 'I'm not seeing visitors!'

'I'm Joe Brook—from the *Daily News*,' Joe said in a loud voice.

A man appeared immediately at the living-room door. He had a bandage round his head. He was very good-looking.

'Come in, Mr Brook,' Gareth Morgan said.

Joe went into the living-room, and Lynn Morgan followed him. The room had some good furniture in it. The chairs were new and comfortable. A modern radio stood beside a large television set. A coal fire was burning in the fire-place.

A little boy was sitting in one of the armchairs. He was doing nothing—just looking into the fire. As soon as Gareth reached the door, he shouted at the child, 'Get up and offer your seat to the gentleman—and then go to bed.'

The little boy got up quickly and ran towards the door. Lynn gently touched the top of his head as he passed. The boy stopped and kissed her.

'He's not our child,' Gareth said. 'He's Polish.'

'Get up and offer your seat to the gentleman.'

'Johnnie *is* our child,' Lynn cried. 'We adopted him.'

Then she left the room.

'That boy's a trouble all the time——' Gareth began.

'I have heard that you were very near the explosion, Mr Morgan,' Joe said quickly. 'I hope your injury is not very bad.'

'Just painful, Mr Brook,' Gareth answered. 'It's one of the risks that we miners have to take.'

Gareth told Joe about the things that happened before and after the explosion. He made jokes about it—and laughed at them himself. He noticed the look on Joe's face.

'You have to laugh in order not to cry,' he said.

'Do you know the cause of the explosion?' Joe asked.

'Oh yes!' Gareth said. 'It was the fault of the manager. The men don't listen to him. They don't take enough care.'

'You don't like Mr Evans?' Joe said.

'No. He's a bad manager,' Gareth replied. 'They ought to sack him.' There was a look of hate on his face as he spoke.

'I've heard that Mr Evans is going to sack *you*,' Joe said.

Gareth gave Joe a quick look. 'Who have you been talking to?' he asked in an angry voice.

'Men at the pit. Talking to people is my job, you know.'

Joe could hear the child crying upstairs. He heard Lynn trying to comfort him.

'That child cries too often!' Gareth complained.

'Why did you adopt him?' Joe asked.

'It was Lynn's idea. The boy's father and mother were killed in a motor accident. The father worked in the same pit as Lynn's father.'

At that moment Lynn came into the room.

'Why are you so cruel to Johnnie?' she said angrily. 'He's unhappy about the accident in the pit—like the rest of us.'

'Mind your own business!' Gareth shouted.

'It is my business!' Lynn cried. 'My brother and his mates are down there. They are all my friends. But they're not your friends. You wouldn't care if they all died. You haven't even volunteered to join a rescue team.'

Gareth jumped to his feet. For a moment Joe thought that he was going to hit his wife.

'Look!' he shouted, pointing at his head.

'You're not hurt at all,' Lynn answered. 'The doctor wouldn't even look at you. Just one little cut. *You* told me to put that bandage round your head!'

Gareth's mouth fell open. He was so angry that he couldn't speak. Lynn continued quietly:

'You're only thinking about Mr Evans. You hate him so much that——'

'Be quiet!' Gareth shouted. He took a step towards his wife.

Lynn did not move. 'You want Mr Evans to die,' she said. 'I can remember your words. You said yesterday, "I hope he'll never come out of the mine alive." '

Gareth looked first at his wife and then at Joe. Then he began to shout. He raised his hand. 'I'll kill you!' he cried.

Joe jumped up and stood between them.

'Get out of my house!' Gareth shouted at Joe.

'No,' said Joe.

'Then *I'll* leave,' Gareth cried. 'But I'll come back!'

He ran out of the room. The front door shut behind him.

'I'm sorry——' Joe began.

'I'll go and see if Johnnie is all right,' Lynn said quickly. 'He's so afraid of Gareth that he can't sleep at night.'

She left the room. A moment later she returned.

'He's gone!' she said. 'Perhaps he has gone to my mother's house. I'll go and see.'

'Shall I come with you?' Joe asked.

'No, thank you,' Lynn said. 'Just leave—and please don't say anything to anybody.'

They left the house together. Joe stood in the street until Lynn had gone into her mother's house. Then he began to walk down the street. He had only taken two steps when a small figure ran out of the shadows. It was Johnnie. He pulled Joe by the arm.

'I want to tell you something. It's very important.'

Joe stopped.

'No, not here!' Johnnie said. 'Father thinks I'm in bed asleep. I got

They climbed the hillside behind the coal tip.

out of the bathroom window. I saw him leave, but he'll come back. He'll see that I've gone, and he'll come and look for me. We must be quick.' He took Joe's hand. 'Come with me.'

Joe went with the boy to the end of the road. Then Johnnie began to run up a narrow path. It climbed the hillside behind the coal tip. The moon had risen, and Joe could see the trees on the skyline far above him. The black sides of the tip hid the Ryddach valley.

They ran through the trees on the hilltop until they reached the edge of the next valley. A narrow path led to the bottom. Joe saw the lights of the houses far below. The town of Maerog was smaller than Ryddach.

Johnnie did not stop, and he did not speak. He ran down the path, and Joe followed him. The path led to an old coal mine. Most of the buildings had fallen down. The shafts were blocked. Piles of bricks and rock and coal covered the ground. Pieces of old iron and broken railway trucks made dark shadows in the moonlight.

Johnnie led Joe to an old brick wall which ran along the side of the hill. He began to pull some of the bricks away.

'Help me,' he said to Joe.

Together Joe and Johnnie threw the bricks to the ground. The moon was shining straight on to the hillside. Through the hole which they had made, Joe saw a wide passage. It led down into the hillside.

Chapter 3

'Where does the passage lead to, Johnnie?' Joe asked.

'I don't know,' Johnnie replied. 'I've never dared to go very far.'

'Then why——?' Joe began.

'I know a lot about mines,' Johnnie said. 'I'm going to be a miner one day. I listen to miners. I think this used to be a way into the Maerog pit. The Maerog pit has been closed for years, but the Ryddach pit is joined to it underground. Miners say that there aren't any proper maps of the Maerog pit.'

'Who else has seen this passage?'

'Nobody. I discovered it—a year ago. I kept it a secret.'

'Why are you showing it to me now?'

'I think it may lead to the trapped miners.'

'Why didn't you tell somebody immediately?'

'I did. I told Father.'

'So Morgan——' Joe cried.

'First he said that I was lying,' Johnnie continued. 'Then he began to shout at me. He said that I mustn't tell anybody—not even Mother. If I did, he would kill me, he said. He also said that he'd kill Mother and then leave the country.'

'But why are you telling *me*?'

'I know that you will help me. I can climb back into my bedroom. Then Father will never know that I showed you. *You* won't tell him.'

Joe looked into the dark passage. 'We'll go straight into Maerog,' he said. 'We'll phone Gwyn Davies. He'll know whether we ought to explore the passage.'

They reached the road and went into the first pub. Johnnie sat quietly in a corner while Joe phoned Gwyn.

Gwyn was excited by Joe's news. 'The boy may be right,' he said.

'U5 District is nearer to Maerog than to Ryddach. And the Maerog valley is deeper than ours. Wait there in the pub. I'll talk to the leader of the rescue team and phone you back.'

'I'm worried about Gareth Morgan,' Joe said. 'You were right. He's dangerous. He hates you all. He may try to look for the passage.'

'Morgan is here at the pit head,' Gwyn said. 'He's wearing his miner's clothes, but he isn't doing anything. He's just watching.'

'Well, watch *him*,' Joe said.

A quarter of an hour later, Gwyn Davies phoned again. He said that there had been another rock fall. The leader of the rescue team was underground. He could not talk to him because the telephone lines in the mine were cut.

'I'm going to bring my own rescue team of volunteers,' he said. 'Morgan is still here. Wait at the pub.'

'Bring a helmet and miner's clothes for me,' Joe said.

While he was waiting, Joe talked to the men in the pub. None of them were miners. Most of them worked in a new steelworks at the bottom of the valley. But the steelworks used Ryddach coal. Many of the workers had friends in Ryddach. They met them in the pubs, and they played football against them.

'There are many miles of roadway under that hill,' one of them said. 'There used to be good coal in the pit, and it was a very safe pit. My father and my uncle used to work in it. If you want any volunteers, I'll come.'

There were cries of 'Me too!' from all round the room. Johnnie sat quietly in his corner and listened.

Twenty minutes later, Gwyn arrived with his rescue team of volunteers. Cliff Williams was among them. Joe put on the clothes and helmet which Gwyn had brought for him.

'Morgan has gone,' Gwyn said quietly to Joe. 'I sent a man to follow him, but Morgan was too clever. We don't know where he is now.'

'We must hurry then,' Joe said.

Johnnie led them. The moon was now hidden behind dark clouds, but the bright lamps of the miners lit up the path.

'I could find my way without a lamp,' Johnnie said. 'I play here during the holidays—when Father is down the mine.'

They were a hundred yards from the hillside when suddenly there was a noise. They stopped and shone their lamps. An old iron wheel was lying on the ground, and dust was rising round it.

'It wasn't the wind,' Joe said. 'There's somebody there!'

'Do you think it was Morgan?' Gwyn asked.

'Yes,' Joe replied. 'We must take care. You ought to tell your men about him.'

'I don't like to do it,' Gwyn said. Then he turned to his team. 'Gareth Morgan may be following us,' he said. 'If you see him, catch him and bring him to me. I want to talk to him.'

'But take care,' Joe added. 'He may have a gun or something.'

They were close to the old railway shed. The building had no roof. It was full of old trucks. Most of them had no wheels. Many of them lay on their sides. The high brick walls all around were full of holes.

'We'll never find him in there,' Joe said.

They followed Johnnie to the hole in the wall. When they reached the passage, Gwyn said, 'What about the boy? We can't take him with us, but we can't leave him here either. Gareth Morgan may come here.'

'You're quite right,' Joe said. 'Perhaps he has been here already. Perhaps he has hidden explosives in the roadway. I'd better go and see. Don't go near the entrance.'

Joe climbed through the hole and began to walk slowly down the roadway. After a few yards the passage was narrower. Joe couldn't stand up straight. The floor was covered with pieces of rock. Water dripped from the roof. He shone his lamp into every hole in the roof and in the walls. Before each step, he looked at the floor with great care. He went fifty yards or more; then he went back to the entrance.

'I couldn't find anything,' he told Gwyn. 'But Morgan may try later—when you're all inside.'

'You think he'll try to kill us all?' Gwyn cried.

'Why not?' Joe replied. 'He wants to kill Ivor Evans. He'll be quite ready to kill other people in order to do that. He's mad.'

'We ought to call the police,' Gwyn said.

'There's isn't time,' said Joe. 'I'll look after Johnnie. I'll also wait for Morgan. Perhaps Cliff Williams could stay with me——'

'Of course,' said Gwyn. 'You won't be alone for long. I've left a message for the leader of the rescue team. As soon as he gets it, he'll come straight here.'

He held up a piece of white chalk.

'I don't know this roadway,' he continued, 'but there will certainly be side roadways. So I'll mark our path.'

'Good-bye, Gwyn,' Joe said in a low voice.

Gwyn's team went into the passage.

'What are we going to do now?' Cliff asked, as soon as the last man had climbed through the hole.

'Turn off your lamp,' Joe said, 'and be as quiet as you can.'

Cliff did so. Joe also turned off his lamp. It was so dark that they could not see their hands in front of their faces. Joe had noticed a large pile of bricks near the entrance. He took Johnnie's hand.

'We'll hide behind the bricks,' he said, 'but don't make any noise.'

They lay down behind the bricks and waited. The sound of footsteps in the passage had gone. A piece of old iron knocked against the wall a few yards away. There were other noises. Joe was worried. He was afraid that he would not hear Gareth coming.

Suddenly a lamp was turned on only a few yards from them. It shone for a few moments on the pile of bricks. Joe and his friends did not dare to breathe. Then the lamp moved towards the entrance of the roadway. They could see the shape of a man.

Joe spoke very quietly to the others: 'Don't move.'

Then he shouted, 'Put your hands up! I've got a gun.'

Gareth Morgan gave a cry of surprise and the lamp shone on the pile of bricks again. Joe did not move. Gareth laughed.

'That's an old trick,' he said. 'I know you haven't got a gun. And I'm carrying gelignite, Mr Brook. You know about gelignite? It's a dangerous explosive—a *very* dangerous explosive.'

'Do you think I'm not ready to die in order to save the lives of fifty men?' Joe said.

'I'm sure you are, Mr Brook. Everybody knows you're a very brave man. But you've got the boy with you.'

Joe felt Johnnie move. He quickly put his hand over the boy's mouth.

'You're wrong, Morgan,' he lied. 'I'm not a fool. I've hidden Johnnie in a safe place. And I don't believe you *are* carrying gelignite. You're not a fool either. You wouldn't dare to carry gelignite.'

At that moment Joe jumped up and turned on his lamp. Gareth was so surprised that he threw back his head. His helmet fell off, and the lamp on it went out. His hands were empty. The light was so bright that he could not see. He turned his eyes away. Then suddenly he ran forward and picked up a brick. He threw it as hard as he could. Joe gave a cry of pain and fell to the ground.

The next moment he felt hands under his arms. He opened his eyes. Cliff was pulling him up, and Johnnie was looking at him anxiously. 'I'm all right,' he said. 'Where's Gareth Morgan?'

'I don't know,' Cliff replied. 'When I turned on my lamp, he had gone.'

They all looked at the black hole in the hillside. Had Gareth Morgan escaped into the mine?

Chapter 4

Joe and Cliff shone their lamps into the entrance. Gareth was not there, but there was a bend in the roadway after ten yards. They listened. There was not a sound.

'It's not safe here,' Joe said. 'If Morgan is still outside, he may come back with the gelignite. He'll take any risk now. I'm quite certain he's mad.'

They moved fifty yards along the wall away from the entrance.

'Take Johnnie back to the pub,' Joe said to Cliff. 'Tell the police. They ought to put up road-blocks. If Morgan escapes he'll try to leave the town—and the country. Then wait for the rescue team. Explain everything to the leader. I'm going to look for Gareth Morgan.'

'I'd rather stay and help you,' said Cliff.

'I'd feel safer with you,' said Johnnie.

'No. You must go—both of you. Turn off your lamp, Cliff, and be as quiet as possible.'

Cliff turned off his lamp, and he and Johnnie moved away into the night. Joe did *not* turn off his lamp. He walked slowly back to the roadway entrance. At every unusual noise he looked round quickly. Those fifty yards seemed like five hundred yards. When at last he reached the entrance, he turned off his lamp. Then he hid again behind the pile of bricks. He waited for five minutes. Nothing happened. The moon had not appeared again from behind the clouds. It began to rain.

Had Gareth Morgan gone down into the mine? It seemed certain that he had. Joe stood up and turned on his lamp. He climbed through the hole in the wall and began to walk. After a hundred yards the roadway got wider again. He went deeper into the mine. He remembered that a miner had once told him: 'If you are lost in a coal mine, always walk towards the wind. It may take you along a long road, but in the end it will bring you to the shaft.' There were no

He had never hunted anyone underground before.

engines to bring air into this empty pit, and there were no longer any shafts.

Joe had explored caves in the Yorkshire hills. He had gone on his hands and knees along many long and narrow passages. But he had never hunted anyone underground before. At every bend in the roadway his heart almost stopped. It was a new kind of fear. Once a piece of rock fell a few yards in front of him, and he threw himself on his face.

At last he reached the first side roadway. Gwyn's chalk marks pointed to the right. There were tram lines in the middle of the right-hand roadway. The left-hand roadway was narrower. A thin seam of coal shone in the light of his lamp. Coal lay among the rocks on the floor.

Joe stood for almost a minute and did not move. There was not a sound. Then he went into the left-hand passage. There was a bend almost immediately. He went round it very slowly. He was ready to jump. 'If Gareth is there,' he thought, 'he won't see me. My lamp will be too bright for him.' But Gareth was *not* there. The road ran straight for twenty yards. Then there was another bend.

Joe's helmet hit the roof at every step. His lamp shone on the floor, but his heavy shoes hit fallen rocks, and he almost fell five or six times. At last he did fall. He was just going to get up when he felt two strong hands on the back of his neck.

A voice said: 'You were not very clever, Mr Brook. I was sure that you'd follow this roadway. So I waited round the corner in the other one. Then I followed you.'

Joe did not move. 'You're finished, Gareth,' he said. 'The police are waiting for you. You can't escape.'

'You're wrong, Mr Brook!' Gareth replied. 'I *am* going to escape. I'm cleverer than them all—I'm cleverer even than Mr Evans. And in five days Mr Evans will be dead!'

'How are you going to kill me?' Joe asked quietly. 'It won't be very difficult. I've broken my leg.'

The lie worked. Just for a moment, Gareth lifted his hands from Joe's neck. Joe gave a great push with his back. Gareth fell over and rolled on to his side. Joe jumped on him, and a great fight began.

Their helmets fell off and their lamps went out. . . .

Gareth was very strong. They rolled from one side of the passage to the other. Their helmets fell off and their lamps went out. It was completely dark, but the fight did not stop. Joe used his feet. Gareth cried out with pain each time one of Joe's heavy shoes hit him. Gareth searched for Joe's eyes with his fingers. The rocks tore their clothes and their bodies. Sweat ran down Joe's face.

Then suddenly a rush of air threw them both to the ground. There was a noise of falling rocks. A part of the roof had fallen. Dust filled Joe's nose and mouth, and he could not breathe.

'Gareth!' he called as soon as he could speak. 'Are you still there?'

'Yes,' said a weak voice.

'Are you hurt?'

'No.'

'The passage is blocked, isn't it? Shall we finish our fight?'

There was no answer.

'Wouldn't you like to kill me before we both die?' Joe asked.

'Don't be a fool!'

'What are you going to do, then?'

'Wait for a rescue team.'

'And wait for the police?'

'I don't want to die down here—like this.'

'Perhaps this passage leads to another roadway?'

'No. It leads to an old coal face.'

'Have you got any matches?'

'No. They've gone. And there may be gas. I'm going to try to find a way over the top of the rock fall.'

'And what will you do if you find it?'

'Wait and see!'

Joe felt the sides of the passage. Then he began to move back from the rock fall. He was afraid that Gareth would throw down rocks from the top. And Gareth did throw rocks. The noise in the passage was terrible. The dust flew. Joe covered his nose and mouth. A few large rocks rolled as far as his feet. Then there was silence.

'Are you still alive, Mr Brook?' Gareth called at last.

Joe did not answer. A stone flew past his ear and hit the wall beyond him.

'You're lucky if you're dead, Mr Brook,' Gareth continued. 'There's not much air in here. We'll die slowly.'

Joe picked up a small stone and threw it as hard as he could towards the voice. There was a cry of pain.

'I'll choose a bigger one next time,' Joe said. 'I can see in the dark.'

'All right,' Gareth said. 'We'll agree that we won't throw stones.'

'What are you going to do now?' Joe asked.

'Tap. If the rock fall is not too thick, the rescue team will hear us. Come and help me.'

'No,' Joe said. 'I'll stay here. You start to tap. When you're tired, I'll take your place.'

Gareth began to tap the passage wall with a piece of rock. He tapped loudly—first three quick taps, then three slow taps. Then he stopped and listened. There was no answering tap. He repeated the taps. He repeated them again and again. The only other sound was the water which dripped from the roof. Joe wondered how much water there was above them in the hillside. For a moment he was terribly afraid. Would the water break through the roof and fill the

42

passage? His mouth was dry. He tried to find the drip, but he failed.

He looked at his watch. The glass was broken. The hands had gone. The minutes passed slowly. Gareth did not speak until he was tired. Then he said, 'Your turn now!'

Gareth touched Joe as he passed. Both men moved quickly away. Neither of them wanted the fight to start again.

But when Joe began to tap, he listened for two noises—an answer to his signal, and a sound from Gareth. Neither noise came. But Gareth understood.

'You're not tapping as hard as you can,' he said. 'You're afraid that I'll attack you, aren't you? Don't worry! I won't hurt you. I need you. Tap harder!'

The hours passed. Joe could not count the number of times he went to the rock face. His tapping got weaker and weaker. So did Gareth's. Breathing was more and more difficult. The two men did not speak at all now. They did not tap any more. They just lay there and waited to die. Joe fell asleep.

He opened his eyes. A light was shining down on him.

'You'll be all right,' a voice said.

'Where am I?' Joe asked.

'Where we found you,' Cliff Williams said. 'We drove an air pipe through to you. Then we started to move the rocks. It took hours.'

'Where's Gareth Morgan?' Joe asked.

'Gareth Morgan?' Cliff cried. 'Was he with you?'

Last miners rescued from Ryddach p
Search continues for Gareth Morga

industry
ne duck."
Minister
try, first
ttack his
he was
of com-
Clyde
Cammell
er have
illions of

ears old,
 disaster
on. Cam-
up on a
contracts.
to huge
 of the
ogramme
ckers at

ve they
uling the
the most
 in the

JCS, Mr
no doubt.
a better
said. Mr
l Laird's
d chief
buoyant.
ut per-
 to pro-
he point
1972 we
ne most
 United
ably in

company
ns is not
ce to the
and its
political

ald prob-
if their
under a
ent. And
manage to
t, it will
ple to be
avour of
approach
aid and
"

Thursday, April 6

All 42 men trapped in the Ryddach pit have now been brought out. None are badly injured. Mr Evans, the mine manager, was the last to leave.

'We were sure we were going to die. Then at 5.30 we heard tapping on the brick wall of a side roadway,' Mr Evans said. 'We thought we were dreaming! We answered the signal and got an immediate reply. We began to pull bricks away. We could hear the rescue team working on the other side. The passage was very narrow. In places it was only three feet high. We had to pull large rocks away in order to make a path. The men were already weak. They knew that the roof could fall at any moment. But they continued to work with great courage.'

Mr Evans praised the courage of the rescue team. Gwyn Davies, leader of the team, said that the chief praise must go to Johnnie Morgan and to Joe Brook. The National Coal Board has already sent them a letter of thanks.

Where is Gareth Morgan? The rescue team searched for him, but they could not find him. Was he hiding in an undiscovered side passage? Nobody knows how he escaped from the Maerog pit. The police want to question him.

'I am sure that Morgan caused the accident,' Mr Evans said. 'I saw him throw something just before the explosion. Then I saw him run.'

Friday, April 7

At 4 o'clock this morning, Gareth Morgan went in through the back door of his house in Cefn Coed Road. Police were hiding in the house. They tried to arrest him, but Morgan took a stick of gelignite from his pocket and lit a fuse.

'If you take one step,' he said, 'I'll destroy the house and everybody in it.'

At that moment a man came into the room and jumped on Morgan from behind. He tore the stick of gelignite from his hand and threw it out of the window. It exploded in the garden. The man was Joe Brook.

'Late on Thursday night,' Mr Brook explained, 'I suddenly had an idea. The police had only just left the Maerog pit, but I decided to have a last look at it myself. I had just reached the entrance when Morgan suddenly appeared. The moon was shining, but he did not see me. His face and clothes were completely black. Clearly he had hidden at the coal face in the passage where we had fought. I'm sure that he was terribly in need of food and water and sleep. But he ran along the wall. The moon went behind a cloud, and I couldn't follow him. But I knew that he would return to his house.'

Morgan is now with the Ryddach police. The police have found a store of gelignite in a hole in the coal tip—less than one hundred yards from the house.

Stu
in

A Caml
tudent vote
of residence
the town's c
The si
tricts, but n
city or large
Even
be in a m

MP
for i
hom

Mr Mich
Labour MP fo
is to ask Mr
for the Envi
emergency act
more families
out of his con
way for Great
housing schen
Mr O'Hall
Walker to di
provide 250 n
site due to h
park off Con
Holloway, Lor
Over 3,000
the area are h
to make way
Alsen and
redevelopment

Exercises—Gold Robbery

1.

Here are six questions on pages 1–2. Four answers follow each question, but only one answer is correct. Write the number of the question and the letter of the correct answer. For the first question you write: '1 C'.

1 Where was the plane flying to?
  It was flying to
    A. Mexico City. *B.* Washington. *C.* New York. *D.* New Orleans.

2 Who took the robbers' cases to the plane?
    A. The chief of the Mexican Police. *B.* Gangsters in police clothes. *C.* Mexican police and airport police. *D.* The guard and the pilot of the plane.

3 The guard saw inside one of the cases. What was in it when it arrived at Mexico City airport?
  It contained
    A. a man and some parachutes. *B.* two men. *C.* two men and some parachutes. *D.* some parachutes.

4 Why didn't the guard shoot the robber?
  He didn't shoot because
    A. the robber shot him. *B.* the second robber shot him. *C.* the second robber hit him. *D.* shooting on a plane isn't safe.

5 How many gold robberies were there before the robbery from the plane?
    A. 5. *B.* More than 5. *C.* More than 4. *D.* 4.

6 Why was Joe Brook angry?
  He was angry because
    A. he had to stay in London. *B.* the robbers had stolen more gold. *C.* he had caused a lot of trouble. *D.* he wanted to see his editor, Dick Clegg.

2.

Look at the first sentence on page 1: 'Last night the gold robbers struck again.' We call *struck* in that sentence a 'verb', but the NAME of the verb is *strike*.

Can you give the NAMES of the verbs in these sentences?

  1 They took the gold from a plane.
  2 The robbers hid themselves on the plane.
  3 The police brought the cases to the airport.
  4 None of their policemen went to the airport.
  5 They have found nothing yet—not even one gold bar.
  6 Joe Brook spent the day in front of a telephone.
  7 Joe Brook never thought about danger.
  8 The police had caught the criminals with Joe's help.
  9 Bob gave himself a large whisky.
  10 The model stood on the table in front of them.

3.

You read this sentence on page 1:

1st VERB   2nd VERB

While the plane was flying through the night, they attacked the guard.

Here are some sentences like that, but you will see a dash (———) for the 1st VERB. Can you write the full sentences?

1 While Mary ——— the letter, the electric light went out.

> (You can have different verbs: *was writing* and *was reading* are both good; *was burning* is possible; but perhaps *was eating* is not very good.)

2 While the pilot ——— his story, the policemen listened.
3 While I ——— tea, the telephone bell rang.
4 While they were ——— the language, their teacher died.
5 While my son ——— the corner, a car struck his bicycle.
6 While Bob ——— a cigarette, Joe noticed his hand.
7 The electric light went out while Mary ——— the letter.
8 The basket broke while I ——— the fruit to the market.
9 The second robber hit him while he ——— at the first robber.

4.

Complete these sentences. Use the past perfect tense, e.g.

> Joe was angry because/Dick Clegg *had refused* to send him to America.

1 Danielle Merveille had sent her photograph to Joe because . . . (p. 3)
2 Joe turned the radio off because . . . (p. 3)
3 Joe was excited because . . . (p. 3)
4 Bob pointed to a Jaguar because . . . (p. 3)
5 Joe cried 'What!' because . . . (p. 3)
6 In the French Quarter, Bob stopped and bent down because . . . (p. 4)
7 In the shop, Bob was surprised because . . . (p. 5)

5.

Make sentences on this pattern (with the second verb in the past perfect tense):

UNCHANGING	2ND SUBJECT	2ND VERB	
Bob told Joe that	the goldsmith	had called	him back.

The facts are on pages 5–6:

	2ND SUBJECT	VERB
1	the goldsmith	offer
2	the goldsmith's hand	go
3	the shop	have
4	a smell of machine-oil	come
5	he	not be able to see
6	he	not say
7	a man	run
8	he	jump

6.

Make sentences which begin: *As soon as . . .*

EXAMPLE Joe jumped up. (p. 6)
Answer: As soon as Bob finished his story, Joe jumped up.

1 Joe looked out of the window. (p. 7)
2 Bob jumped into the taxi. (p. 7)
3 Joe ran towards the girl. (p. 7)
4 The girl walked away. (p. 8)
5 A violent quarrel started. (p. 8)
6 Carlo walked away towards Piccadilly. (p. 8)
7 Joe ran down the steps after him. (p. 9)

7.

Complete the relative clause in each sentence.

EXAMPLE Piccadilly Circus was full of Scotsmen who . . . (p. 9)
Answer: Piccadilly Circus was full of Scotsmen who had come to London to see a football game.

1 The stick which . . . was at home. (p. 10)
2 The face that . . . was very ugly. (p. 10)
3 The man who . . . had no hair. (p. 10)
4 Angus gave guns to the men who . . . (p. 11)
5 Angus Macfarlane looked at the model that . . . (p. 12)
6 The man who . . . was clearly Menodotti. (p. 12)
7 The FBI knew the name of the man who . . . (p. 13)

8.

The dash takes the place of one word:

When	Where	Who	Which	Why

What is the full question?

1 —— is the head of the gang?—The police don't know his name.
2 —— was there a guard on the plane?—Because there was gold in it.
3 —— did Danielle Merveille send Joe a photograph?—After he had saved her from a snake.
4 —— had Bob found the model?—In a New Orleans street.
5 —— building was it a model of?—The Empire State Building.
6 —— heard Bob when he cried out?—A policeman.
7 —— didn't the man in the shop bring out his gun?—Because the policeman was there.
8 —— was the man's gun?—It was in his pocket.
9 —— will you write the letter?—Tomorrow, perhaps.
10 —— photograph was the best one?—The photograph of Danielle Merveille, I think.

9.

Take this sentence to pieces:
The robbers hid themselves on the plane at Mexico City.

Here are my pieces:
     on the plane
     hid
     at Mexico City
     the robbers
     themselves

Now here are my pieces of other sentences. Can you put the sentences together?
(* means: Please don't put this first.)

1 to the airport
   hurt
  *on the way
   myself
   I

2 himself
   in hospital
   found
   the guard
   in a bed

3 for the accident
   ourselves
   we
   at the corner
   blamed

4 yourself
  *with this camera
   can photograph
   you
   quite easily

5 of the bridge
   he
   over the side
   himself
   threw

6 the little girl
   in the kitchen
   herself
   under the table
   hid

7 destroyed
   the old ship
   near the island
   on the rocks
   itself

8 *at tea time
   yourselves
   you
   this afternoon
   must look after

9 himself
   unwisely filled
   from the kitchen
   table
   the fat boy
   with food

10.

Did you notice these words on page 1: 'One of the policemen showed me papers'?
Make some more sentences like that:

1	2	3	4	5
One of the	girls men pilots	gave	us the children everybody	some presents a drink advice

Which box (Box 2, Box 4, or Box 5) could you put these in?

1 policeman (Answer: [Box] 2)

2 me
5 help
8 their meal

3 teachers
6 somebody
9 gentlemen

4 some money
7 our friends
10 each boy

11.

Four replies:

                    I think so. (= Yes, I do. But I'm not sure.)
                    I don't think so. (= No, I don't. But I'm not sure.)

Do you know the answer?	*I'm afraid so.* (= Yes.—I'm sorry that that is the answer.)
	I'm afraid not. (= No.—I'm sorry that that is the answer.)

Give us one of the 4 replies:

1 'Is my nose shining?' (Yes.)
2 'Is he an honest man?' (Yes.)
3 'Was the car going too fast?' (No.)
4 'Is there a letter for me from my girl friend?' (No.)
5 'Am I in danger?' (Yes.)
6 'Is her telephone number 01–222–0471?' (Yes.)
7 'Will she be rude to me?' (No.)
8 'Will she be rude to me?' (Yes.)
9 'Is she always rude to everybody?' (No.)
10 'I want to be rude to her. May I?' (No.)

12.

> No reporter had had so many UNUSUAL adventures.

Put the right word into the space:

comfortable/uncomfortable	Nobody likes —— chairs. I sleep best in —— beds.
true/untrue	It's —— that the Thames flows through London. If I tell a lie, it's ——.
safe/unsafe	I'm afraid this bicycle is ——. Haven't you got a —— one?
familiar/unfamiliar	We came by —— roads. By —— roads, we can get here in less time.
happily/unhappily	We were singing ——. But —— our car struck a
necessary/unnecessary	stone. The —— accident made us angry. It is never —— to leave big stones in the road.
important/unimportant	If there are any —— letters, I will answer them immediately. But —— letters can wait until Saturday.
kind/unkind	Does that seem ——? I want to be —— to everybody, but I haven't got time to write letters.

13.

The right verb in the right form:

send   bring

1 Bob had —— Joe a card from New Orleans.
2 Mary came to see me and —— her new boy friend.
3 He would have —— the gun out of his pocket if the policeman hadn't been there.
4 'The editor never —— me to exciting places,' he said.
5 He said that the editor never —— him to exciting places.

49

do   make

6 Betty —— some coffee for me last night.
7 I must —— my work before breakfast.
8 The policemen were only —— their duty.
9 You're learning English, are you? Will you ever —— use of the language?
10 You've been to England, have you? Did you —— any business there?

say   tell

11 He —— me to go away, but I refused.
12 I —— that I was going away, but it wasn't true.
13 Did he —— the words 'I love you'?
14 Who —— I'm lying?
15 —— me that you love me.

14.

must   ought to   needn't

A policeman	*must* be ready to help people.
He	*ought to* try to catch criminals.
He	*needn't* be able to repair a car.

Can you make more sentences like those? What else *must* a policeman do? What else *ought* he to do? What else *needn't* he do?

Now try to make *must*, *ought to*, *needn't* sentences about these people.

1 A driver *must* ...
   He   *ought to* . . .
   He   *needn't* . . .

2 A reporter   3 A doctor   4 An artist
5 A detective   6 An editor   7 A gangster
8 A goldsmith   9 A father   10 A teacher

15.

Words that join sentences.

Joe Brook never thought about danger   there was a good story.

                                        ↑

Does this make a good sentence? ⟶ *when*   Yes.
Does this? ————————————⟶ *if*   Yes.
And this? ———————————————⟶ *until*   Well, yes. But it isn't true.
And this? ——————————⟶ *because*   No.

Try these:

1 I always have a drink   I'm thirsty.
      (until—because—if—when—where)
2 They never ask questions   they know the answers.
      (when—until—if—unless—because)
3 They'll find nothing   they search the ship.
      (because—until—if—unless—when)

4 I am quite certain   I made no mistake.
  (if—because—that—until—unless)
5 The gunfight ended   Hyman Dixon showed a white flag.
  (until—if—because—that—when)
6 Joe told his story   the doctor was working on his wound.
  (when—where—because—while—unless)

Exercises—Mine Mystery

1.

Here are eight questions on page 35. Four answers follow each question, but only one answer is correct. Write the number of the question and the letter of the correct answer. For the first question you write '1 A'.

1 How many men did not escape at the time of the explosion?
  A. 57. *B.* 59. *C.* 13. *D.* 54.

2 Where was Mr Hemmings at the time of the explosion?
  A. He was in the mine office. *B.* He was in his own office. *C.* He was in the mine, a few yards from the coal face. *D.* He was in the mine, with one of the rescue teams.

3 Who saw Mr Evans pull Mr Hemmings back?
  A. One of the three dead men. *B.* One of the men who were able to leave the mine. *C.* One of the men who were trapped at the coal face. *D.* One of the 42 other miners.

4 Which of the answers is the same as: 'I had to run for my life'?
  A. I had never run so fast before. *B.* I wanted to run but I could not move. *C.* If I had not run, I would have saved Mr Evans and Mr Hemmings. *D.* If I had not run, the falling rock would have killed me.

5 Which of these is true?
  A. There had been no bad accidents in Welsh coal mines for 20 years. *B.* There had been one other bad accident in a Welsh coal mine, 20 years before. *C.* There is a bad accident in a Welsh coal mine every 20 years. *D.* There have been Welsh coal mines for 20 years and this was the first bad accident.

6 Why did Mr Hemmings receive a cold welcome?
  A. Because he arrived at Ryddach in the morning. *B.* Because people wanted to ask him unpleasant questions. *C.* Because the NCB wanted to close Ryddach. *D.* Because there were too many modern machines in the pit.

7 Who knew the cause of the explosion?
  A. The miner who hit a reporter. *B.* The reporter who asked unpleasant questions. *C.* Nobody. *D.* People who know miners.

8 The rescue teams had to
  A. Make a new shaft to reach the trapped men. *B.* Make a way through the rock and earth in the main roadway. *C.* Promise to reach the trapped men in three days—perhaps four. *D.* Use their safety lamps to find the gas in the roadway.

2.

Complete these sentences. Use the past perfect tense, e.g.
> The miners could not get out because/explosions *had blocked* the roadways in the pit.

1 Mr Hemmings and Mr Evans were in the pit because . . . (p. 35)
2 Some miners treated a reporter roughly because . . . (p. 35)
3 Joe Brook was in Ryddach because . . . (p. 36)
4 One man was on a stretcher because . . . (p. 37)
5 The men of the rescue team shook their heads because . . . (p. 37)
6 At the time of the explosion Cliff was not working because . . . (p. 38)
7 The boy was dead because . . . (p. 39)
8 Cliff and his mate ran for their lives because . . . (p. 39)
9 Gwyn Davies recognised Joe because . . . (p. 39)
10 Gwyn knew about the life of a miner because . . . (p. 40)

3.

Make sentences on this pattern (with the second verb in the past perfect tense):

UNCHANGING	2ND SUBJECT	2ND VERB	
Gwyn told Joe that	the NCB	had provided	pit-head baths.

The facts are on page 42

	2ND SUBJECT	VERB
1	a trouble-maker	marry
2	Morgan and his wife	adopt
3	Gareth	win
4	the smaller schoolboys	fear
5	Gareth's gang of schoolboys	destroy
6	the police	catch
7	the police	never catch
8	Gareth	quarrel
9	Gareth	find
10	Gareth's Ryddach gang	damage

4.

Make sentences which begin: *As soon as* . . .

EXAMPLE Joe recognised her. (p. 43)
> *Answer:* As soon as the young woman opened the door, Joe recognised her.

1 Gareth appeared at the sitting-room door. (p. 44)
2 Gareth shouted at Johnnie. (p. 44)
3 Johnnie stopped and kissed her. (p. 44)
4 Lynn left the room. (p. 45)
5 Gareth jumped up. (p. 45)
6 Joe jumped up. (p. 46)
7 Lynn interruped Joe. (p. 46)
8 Joe began to walk down the street. (p. 46)
9 Johnnie began to run up a narrow path. (p. 47)
10 He began to pull some loose bricks away. (p. 47)

5.

Answer the questions; include *used to* in the words you use.

1 What was the passage at one time? (p. 48)
2 Where did the Maerog men meet the Ryddach men? (p. 49)
3 What games did they play? (p. 49)
4 What was the quality of the Maerog coal? (p. 49)
5 How did Johnnie learn the way through the Maerog pit buildings? (p. 50)

6.

Look at this sentence from page 36: 'He had flown straight to Cardiff.' We call *had flown* in that sentence a 'verb', but the NAME of the verb is *fly*.

Can you give the names of the verbs in these sentences?

1 The mine lay at the bottom of a deep valley.
2 Not far from the entrance, the passage bent to the left.
3 The dark coal tip rose like a mountain.
4 He lost his son during the war, and now he has lost his grandson.
5 His body was brought out this morning.
6 The mates of the man on the stretcher shook their heads.
7 Joe Brook understood the woman's silence.
8 One of the men had forgotten something.
9 A few moments later, we felt a rush of air.
10 Cliff Williams lit another cigarette.

7.

An important little word after the verb.

Joe looked   the young woman with surprise.
Joe *looked at* the young woman with surprise.

Can you add the little words in these?

1 Some of the miners quarrelled   some reporters.
2 The rescue teams were searching   their friends.
3 Did Joe Brook agree   Gwyn Davies?
4 The women were waiting   news from the mine.
5 Joe Brook left London at 11.30. His plane arrived   Cardiff airport at 13.45.
6 The reporters wanted news and were ready to pay   it.
7 He asked   silence, and they listened   him.
8 The miners are fighting   better pay.

8.

'Odd man out'—One of these words doesn't belong to the list—it's the *odd man out*.

car, ambulance, bridge, plane (*bridge* is the odd man out—it isn't a machine)

Which is the odd man out? Why?

1 rescuer, team, reporter, miner
2 pick, spoon, knife, fork
3 wood, coal, water, gas

4 brave, intelligent, mad, clever
5 dead, kill, hurt, injure
6 table, furniture, chair, armchair

9.

The right verb in the right form:

send   bring

1 The editor had —— Joe Brook to Ryddach.
2 The great wheel was turning. It was —— up the cage.
3 His mates —— the man out of the cage on a stretcher.
4 Morgan's father —— him to the grammar school.
5 Why is he —— his son to bed?

carry   take

6 Joe left the house and —— a few steps towards the mine.
7 I have to —— my car to the garage.
8 She bought a lot of things in the shop and —— them here.
9 I've —— six photographs of this house.
10 When I saw her on the road, she was —— a basket.

put on   wear

11 I'm just —— my shoes. Please wait for me.
12 When she came into the room, she was —— a blue dress.
13 She —— her best dress at 2 o'clock and left the house at 2.05.
14 You'll know me because I'll be —— a red flower in my hair.
15 What shall I —— at the party tonight?

10.

Take this sentence to pieces:
    Most of them worked in a new steelworks at the bottom of the valley.

Here are my pieces:
        of the valley
        in a new steelworks
        worked
        most of them
        at the bottom

Now here are my pieces of other sentences. Can you put the sentences together?
(* = Please don't put this first.)

1 lived
  of the tip
  near the foot
  in the old house
  many of the men

2 some of the boys
  at the end
  from the village
  of the road
  came

3 in the sheds
  was
  of the railway line
  most of the coal
  at the side

4 *for the fourth time
  a few of the rescuers
  that day
  into the mine
  went down

5 stayed
  until the end
  none of the men
  in the passage
  of the day

6 of the line
  off the trucks
  a lot of the coal
  fell
  on to the side

54

7 *on the road	8 in those days	9 part of the mine
of the mine	most people	towards the town
was standing alone	of the life	in the next valley
*outside the gate	have no idea	of Maerog
one of the women	of a miner	ran

11.

'He'd like to talk to the great Joe Brook' (page 41).
Begin these with either *I would like to* [Say: *I'd like to*] or *I wouldn't like to*.

1 see Naples before I die.
2 be weak and ill when I'm old.
3 be a miner even in a modern mine.
4 have a fight underground.
5 marry a good-looking man (or woman).
6 go to Mandalay while I'm young.

12.

You read this sentence on page 52:

        1st VERB   2nd VERB
        When I turned on my lamp, he had gone.

Here are some sentences like that, but you will see a dash (——) for the 2nd VERB.
Can you write the full sentences?

1 When Cliff Williams got up after his fall, his lamp ——.

    (You can have different verbs: *had broken* and *had gone out* are both good; *had failed* is possible; but perhaps *had died* is not very good.)

2 When we reached the top of the hill, the moon ——.
3 When the ambulance arrived, she —— a bandage round his head.
4 When Joe looked for them, the miners —— to the shower room.
5 When the police saw him, he —— a stick of gelignite.
6 When Morgan threw a stone, Joe —— to safety.
7 It was 6.30 a.m. and the sun —— when we came out of the shaft.
8 Morgan —— at the coal face when the police searched the pit.
9 We were too late. The train —— when we arrived at the station.

13.

This is Gwyn Davies's story with some words left out. The words are:

*ambulance	*block	*bring	cage
district	explosion	face	government
*helmet	*injure	inspector	main
manager	*phone	pit	rescue
*rescuer	shaft	team	*trap

Put one of the words in the place of each dash (——). If the word has the sign *, you must change its form ('*helmet' will be 'helmets'; '*phone' will be 'phoned', &c.).
Use each word once only.

Hemmings, the ―― ――, arrived at 9 o'clock. Evans, the ――, was waiting for him. They put ―― on their heads and walked over to the ―― head. They went down into the mine in the ――. Five minutes later they ―― to me from the ―― roadway and said that they were going to the coal ―― in the U4 ――.

At 10.35 the telephone rang again. I heard Cliff Williams's voice. He said that there had been an ―― and that a large number of men were ――.

I gave the accident signal immediately, and in five minutes the first ―― ―― was on the way down the ――. The police arrived very quickly and allowed only doctors' cars and ―― to drive in through the gates.

The first report reached me at 11. A heavy fall of rock had ―― the roadway. The ―― had found the bodies of three men and they were ―― ten ―― men up on stretchers.

14.

Did you notice these words: 'The National Coal Board has sent them a letter of thanks'?

Make more sentences like that:

1	2	3	4	5	6
The	newspaper government Hospital Board	has	sent given offered	me somebody my friend	a lot of money some advice nothing

Which box (Box 2, Box 5 or Box 6) could you put these in?

1 us (Answer: [Box] 5)   2 manager
3 all the men   4 £40
5 a present   6 secretary
7 Joe Brook   8 a television set
9 the manager   10 his wife

Now read Bush Fire and Hurricane Paula by Richard Musman. Two more Joe Brook stories at L.S.R. Stage 5.

Glossary

admirer [əd'maiərə], a person who *admires* another person, i.e. thinks that he or she is wonderful.

adopt [ə'dɔpt], take as (your) own. *Johnnie's father and mother are dead, and we have adopted him; he is our adopted son.*

agent ['eidʒənt], a person who acts for another; a *special agent* of the FBI is a *detective* (see below).

ambulance ['æmbjuləns], a large car with beds for sick people.

anxious ['æŋkʃəs], afraid of the things that may happen; troubled in thought; n. **anxiety** [æŋ'zaiəti].

arch [ɑːtʃ], a curve at the top of a door, window or other opening.

archway ['ɑːtʃwei], an opening in a wall; its top is an *arch* = a curve of brick or stone.

arrest [ə'rest], stop (somebody) and hold (him), as the police do.

artist ['ɑːtist], a person who paints pictures or makes other beautiful things.

Aston Martin ['æstn 'mɑːtin], a make of fast car.

bandage ['bændidʒ], a long narrow piece of cloth to tie over a cut.

baseball ['beisbɔːl], an American game.

believe [bi'liːv], think that (something) is true.

bend (*I bent it; I have bent it*) /bend, bent/ change shape; a *bend* in a road, &c., is a curve or corner.

bitter ['bitə], feeling sad and angry.

block [blɔk], fill a road, &c., so that people cannot pass; at a *road-block* the police stop all cars, &c., and look into them; all the buildings between one street and the next.

blood [blʌd]—*Blood* flows through our bodies from our hearts.

board, *on board* = on a boat, ship or plane.

brass [brɑːs], yellow metal made by mixing two other metals (it is of much less value than gold).

bullet ['bulit], a shot from a gun; **bullet-proof** ['bulitpruːf] = made to stop bullets and save the life of the person inside.

bully ['buli], a man or boy who makes weaker people unhappy and enjoys his power.

cabin ['kæbin], a small room in a boat, &c. *We had a very comfortable cabin on the Queen Elizabeth II.*

cage [keidʒ], a box-like car which carries miners, coal, &c., between the top and the bottom of a mine.

cave [keiv], a big hole in rock, especially in the side of a hill.

Cefn Coed ['kevən 'kɔid].

Chicago [ʃi'kɑːgəu].

club [klʌb], a number of people joined together because they like the same things; the building in which they meet.

coal [kəul], black rock-like material which burns; the *coal face* is the part of a mine where the coal is.

collect [kə'lekt], get and keep together, e.g. *Some people collect stamps.*

complain [kəm'plein], say that you don't like (something).

conveyer belt [kən'veiə belt], a long piece of leather (&c.) without ends—a machine makes it move round to carry things. *At the airport they put your bags on a conveyer belt—and you hope that you will see them again.*

crime [kraim], doing wrong, e.g. *Robbery is a crime*; a man who lives by crime is a **criminal** ['kriminl].

curtain ['kɔːtn], a piece of cloth that covers a window.

Dai [dai].

deal with ['diːl wið], do the necessary thing(s) to; to *deal with* a person may be to kill him.

district ['distrikt], a part of a mine, &c.

docks [dɔks], places where big ships load and unload. The sides of the docks are **quays** [kiːz]. *The London docks have 48 miles of quays.*

drip [drip], (of water) fall slowly.

earthquake ['əːθkweik], a change of

place of rocks under the ground, causing the earth to move in a dangerous way.

editor ['editə], the person who decides the place of reports, &c., in a newspaper; he gives orders to the reporters.

entrance ['entrəns], the way into a place.

explode [iks'pləud], break into pieces with a loud noise and a rush of air. If you use matches near an **explosive** [iks'pləusiv] gas, the result is an **explosion** [iks'pləuʒn]. We use **explosives** [iks'pləusivz] like gelignite to break up rocks.

faint [feint], be suddenly unable to see, feel, &c., because one is so weak.

fair [fɛə], with light (not dark) hair.

FBI ['efbiː'ai], (Federal Bureau of Investigation) the police office for all the United States; it investigates (= finds out about) crimes which are not the business of the police of only one state.

field-glasses ['fiːldɡlɑːsiz], glasses for both eyes to make distant things seem near.

finger-prints ['fiŋɡəprints], marks of a person's fingers which help the police to discover criminals.

fireman ['faiəmən], a man who tries to stop fires in burning buildings and to save lives.

Fleet Street ['fliːt striːt], the London street which has most of the newspaper offices in it.

funnel ['fʌnl], the round metal part that the smoke from a ship's engine-room fires passes through.

furniture ['fəːnitʃə], chairs, tables, &c.

fuse [fjuːz], something which causes an explosive to explode at a chosen time.

gang [ɡæŋ], a number of men who work together. very often in crime: **gangster** ['ɡæŋstə] = one of a *gang* of criminals.

Gareth ['ɡæreθ].

gelignite ['dʒelignait], a kind of explosive (see *explode* above).

glad—*Glad to know you* = I am

pleased to meet you.

Glamorgan [ɡlə'mɔːɡən].

gold [ɡəuld], yellow metal of great value; **goldsmith** ['ɡəuldsmiθ] = a man who makes things of gold; a *goldsmith's* (*shop*) = a shop which sells and repairs things made of gold.

grammar school ['ɡræmə skuːl], a school for 12–18-year-old pupils. *Some of the grammar schools in England took their first pupils more than 500 years ago.*

guy [ɡai], (American) a fellow.

hall [hɔːl], a very large room.

handkerchief ['hæŋkətʃif], a square piece of cloth that we carry in a pocket.

Haymarket ['heimɑːkit].

helmet ['helmit], a metal hat. *Soldiers, miners, builders and other workers wear helmets of different kinds.*

hospital ['hɔspitl], a big building for sick people.

independence [indi'pendəns], being free, and not taking orders from other people.

injure ['indʒə], hurt (a person's body, e.g. break his leg, or make deep cuts, &c.); n. *injury* ['indʒəri].

inspect [in'spekt], look at (something) in order to be sure that it is right (e.g. working properly, &c.); an *inspector* [in'spektə] looks at work, &c., and makes a report on it.

intelligent [in'telidʒənt], quick to learn.

Jaguar ['dʒæɡjuə], a make of fast car.

Japanese [dʒæpə'niːz].

joke [dʒəuk], something that a person says in order to make other people laugh.

Kensington ['kenziŋtən].

kid [kid], a child (familiar, especially US).

laboratory [lə'bɔrətri]—Police *laboratories* make tests to find out the facts about things.

lock [lɔk], a metal thing that keeps a door shut; when you *lock* the door, other people cannot open it.

Louisiana [luːiːzi'ænə].

lucky ['lʌki], get good results by chance.

Lynn [lin].

mad [mæd], ill in the *brain* (= the part inside our heads which makes us act with reason). A *mad* elephant behaves in an unusual and dangerous way.

Maerog ['mairɔg].

main [mein], biggest, most important, &c.

manager ['mænidʒə], man who gives orders to all the workers.

mate [meit], a fellow worker (man); a friend (man) at work.

mean [miːn]—*I mean* = that is the idea that I want to give you.

Mexico, Mexican ['meksikəu, 'meksikn].

mind [maind]—*Mind your own business* = This is not your problem, so don't push yourself into it.

missing ['misiŋ]—If a person is *missing*, others have been unable to find him.

model ['mɔdl], a thing that is the same shape as another but smaller. *My model railway engine is only 10 centimetres long.*

mould [məuld], a container which gives shape to metal (the hot metal gets cool and takes the shape of the *mould*).

National Coal Board ['næʃnl 'kəul bɔːd], the body which is in charge of all British coal mines; we often call it the NCB ['ensiː'biː].

Negro ['niːgrəu], a man of the African people who are dark in colour.

New Orleans [njuː 'ɔːliənz].

nickel ['nikl], silvery-white metal; *nickel-plated* = with a thin coat of nickel (the *plating* is usually done by electricity).

night-club ['naitklʌb], a place where people can eat and drink, dance, and watch dancers, &c., after restaurants are shut.

notice—To *take no notice* = to seem not to see or hear (somebody).

object ['ɔbdʒikt], a thing that you can see or touch.

Pall Mall ['pæl'mæl].

passage ['pæsidʒ], a narrow way with a wall on each side.

pavement ['peivmənt], the raised part at the side of a street for people on foot. (In the United States it is called the *sidewalk*.)

Piccadilly [pikə'dili]—The street called Piccadilly meets four other streets at **Piccadilly Circus** ['pikədili 'səːkəs].

pipe [paip]—Water comes to your house through a metal *pipe*.

pick [pik], a *pickaxe* for breaking up rock, &c.

pit [pit], a mine; the *pit head* is the top of the hole which goes down into the mine, with the buildings above it.

poster ['pəustə], a big piece of paper which names the most important news. *The posters said 'TERRIBLE RAILWAY ACCIDENT', so I bought the* Evening News.

praise [preiz], say that (something or somebody) is very good, &c.; n. *praise. The captain praised all his men. 'They were all very brave,' he said.*

prisoner ['prizənə], a person who is not free (the police or other people have put him in a place that he cannot leave).

prove [pruːv], show that something is true.

pub [pʌb], a *public house* where anybody over the age of 18 can buy a drink. *The miners meet at the pub in the evening for a glass of beer, a talk and perhaps a game.*

quarter ['kwɔːtə], a part of a city. *People from France built their houses long ago in the French Quarter of New Orleans.*

quay [kiː]—see *docks* above.

reporter [ri'pɔːtə], a man or woman who writes reports for a newspaper.

rescue [reskjuː], save from danger. Men who *go to the rescue* of others are **rescuers** ['reskjuəz]; rescuers work together in a group called a **rescue team** ['reskjuː tiːm].

respect [ri'spekt], show that you see the special value of (another person).

risk [risk], accept danger; *risk your life* = go into great danger where something may kill you; n. a *risk*.

rob [rɔb]—To *rob* another person = to take his money, &c., by force; a man who robs others is a **robber** ['rɔbə]; his crime is **robbery** ['rɔbəri].

rope [rəup], a very thick, strong line to tie a ship to the quay, or to pull heavy things up, &c.

row [rəu], a line, e.g. a *row of houses*, all close together and side by side.

rub [rʌb], use force to move something (e.g. a dry cloth) forwards and back on another thing. *We rub some things when we want to make them shine.*

run—*Run for your life* = Run fast in order to escape from great danger.

Ryddach ['ri:ðæx].

sabotage ['sæbətɑ:ʒ], destroying machines, &c., in a place of work. *The men broke our newest machine today; it was sabotage, not an accident.*

sack [sæk], tell (a person) that there is no more work (for him).

safety ['seifti], being safe; a miner's **safety lamp** ['seifti læmp] shows when there is dangerous gas, but it cannot cause an *explosion* (see *explode* above).

sale [seil], selling; if we want to sell something, it is *for sale*.

scar [skɑ:], a mark in the place of an old cut on a person's body.

Scotland Yard ['skɔtlənd 'jɑ:d], the central offices of the London police.

seam [si:m], a line of coal running through rock. *The coal seams of today were the forest floors of the distant past.*

seize [si:z], take by force.

secretary ['sekrətri], a person who does the office work (for the manager of a coal mine). *The mine secretary is an important man; he has his own secretary—Miss Jones.*

shaft [ʃɑ:ft], a hole going straight down into a mine (like a well).

shake (*I shook it; I have shaken it*) [ʃeik—ʃuk—'ʃeikn], cause (something) to move quickly from side to side or up and down; *shake your head* = move your head in the sign for 'No'.

shed [ʃed], a store building without rooms. *The farmer keeps his tractors and other machines in a big shed.*

shock [ʃɔk], the result of a terrible surprise. *Doctors advise us to give a warm sweet drink and complete rest to a person with shock.*

shower ['ʃauə], a *shower-bath* in which water falls on you like rain.

sidewalk ['saidwɔ:k]—see *pavement* above.

silent ['sailənt], without a sound; n. **silence** ['sailəns].

skyscraper ['skaiskreipə], a very tall building. *The skyscrapers of New York are famous; the Empire State Building is one of them.*

slip [slip], move too easily by accident. *My feet slipped on the ice, and I fell heavily.*

Soho ['səuhəu].

state [steit], a country, or an important part of a country. *In 1959 a 50th state was added to the United States of America—Hawaii.*

steel [sti:l], the strong metal (for machines, knives, &c.) that we make from iron; steel is made in a *steelworks*.

sticking-plaster ['stikiŋplɑ:stə], a small piece of material which sticks to our body to cover a cut.

stretcher ['stretʃə], strong cloth between two long pieces of wood; two men can carry a sick person on this.

strike (*I struck; I have struck*) [straik—strʌk], hit with force. *The robbers struck again* = they took more gold.

suitcase ['sju:tkeis], a bag (with hard sides) for your clothes when you are travelling.

sure [ʃuə]—*Sure!* = Yes, of course (mostly US).

sweat [swet]—We *sweat* when we are very hot; we get wet with our own *sweat*.

tap [tæp], knock (with the hand or a stick, stone, &c.) on something: n. *tap* = the short sound that tapping once will make.

team, *rescue team*—see *rescue*.

tempt [tempt], try to make (somebody) want something, especially something that he ought not to want.

thirties ['θəːtiz], *the thirties* = the years 1930–1939.

tip [tip], a pile (sometimes a large hill) made out of the waste material (rock, &c.) from a coal mine.

top secret ['tɔp 'siːkrit], very secret; *Top Secret* on important papers = do not show these papers to anybody else.

Trafalgar Square [trə'fælgə 'skwɛə].

tram [træm], a number of small cars on rails (**tram lines** ['træm lainz]) like narrow railway lines.

trapped [træpt], caught, and not able to escape from a place.

trick [trik], something that you do in order to give other people the wrong idea. *He lay on the ground like a dead man, but it was a trick: he was alive.*

tub [tʌb], a small bath made of wood or iron.

underground ['ʌndəgraund], below the ground; *the Underground* = the railways which run under the streets and buildings of London; down in the mine.

uniform ['juːnifɔːm], special clothes, the same for all the men (or women) in a group.

vest [vest], a piece of clothing to cover a man's body. (British English uses *vest* for a piece of clothing worn under the shirt; an American *vest* has buttons and goes outside the shirt.)

violent ['vaiələnt], very hard; in a *violent quarrel* both people are very angry indeed.

volunteer ['vɔlən'tiə], offer to do something. *The captain called for volunteers to do the dangerous work, and every man volunteered.*

Wembley ['wembli].

West End ['west 'end]—The *West End* of London is the part with the big shops, the well-known parks, &c.

whisky ['wiski], a strong drink from Scotland, or (**whiskey** ['wiski]) from Ireland, &c.

winding-tower ['waindiŋ tauə], a metal *tower* (= high narrow building) at the top of a mine *shaft* (see above); it usually has a large wheel for the steel line which pulls (winds) the *cage* up.

work—*The lie worked* = . . . gave the result that the speaker hoped to see.

workshop ['wəːkʃɔp], a place where people repair or make things, using machines. *My car's in the workshop because it hit a lamp-post.*

worried ['wʌrid], troubled in thought; afraid.

wound [wuːnd], a place where something has hurt our body, especially a deep cut; to *wound* = to cause a wound.

Some titles in this series:
1. Recommended for use with children (aged 8–12)
2. Recommended for use with young people (aged 12–15)
3. Recommended for use with older people (aged 15 plus)
   No figure: recommended for use with all ages

Stage 4

The Prisoner of Zenda
  Anthony Hope
Silas Marner
  George Eliot (2.3)
The Thirty-Nine Steps
  John Buchan
Seven Greek Tales
  A.M. Nashif
Gold Robbery and Mine Mystery
  Richard Musman (2.3)
The Angry Valley
  Nigel Grimshaw (2.3)
Island of the Blue Dolphins
  Scott O'Dell
The White Mountains
  John Christopher (2.3)
The Birds and other short stories
  Daphne du Maurier (2.3)
The Forger
  Robert O'Neill (2.3)
Fast Circuit
  Bruce Carter (2.3)
Désirée, the Wife of Marshal Bernadotte
  Annemarie Selinko (2.3)
Doomwatch: The World in Danger
  K. Pedler and G. Davis
Me, Myself and I:
  Seven Science Fiction Stories
  Asimov, Clarke, Tenn etc. (3)
How Happily She Laughs and other
  poems
  Ed. Ian Serraillier

Plays

Three Mystery Plays
  Donn Byrne
Loyalty
  Richard Musman

Non-Fiction

Oil
  Norman Wymer (2.3)
What's Happening in Medicine
  J.H. Dent

Stage 5

Kidnapped
  R.L. Stevenson
The Adventures of Tom Sawyer
  Mark Twain
The Sign of Indra
  Nigel Grimshaw (2)
On the Beach
  Nevil Shute (2.3)
Stranger Things Have Happened
  Susan Bennett (2.3)
Mogul
  John Elliot (2.3)
Bush Fire and Hurricane Paula
  Richard Musman (2.3)
The Diamond as Big as the Ritz
  and other stories
  F. Scott Fitzgerald (2.3)
The Bike Racers
  Bruce Carter (2.3)
The City of Gold and Lead
  John Christopher (2.3)
Désirée, Queen of Sweden
  Annemarie Selinko (2.3)
Wild Jack
  John Christopher (2.3)
Hard Times
  Charles Dickens (2.3)

Plays

The Seventh Key
  Lewis Jones and Michael Smee (2.3)
Mystery on the Moor
  Lewis Jones and Michael Smee (2.3)
Inspector Thackeray Investigates
  Kenneth James and Lloyd Mullen (2.3)

Non-Fiction

Animals Dangerous to Man
  Richard Musman (2.3)
Man and Modern Science
  Norman Wymer (2.3)